THE HUMAN ELEMENT IN
THE MAKING OF A CHRISTIAN

THE HUMAN ELEMENT IN THE MAKING OF A CHRISTIAN

STUDIES IN PERSONAL EVANGELISM

BY

BERTHA CONDÉ

SENIOR STUDENT SECRETARY FOR THE NATIONAL BOARD OF YOUNG WOMEN'S
CHRISTIAN ASSOCIATIONS

NEW YORK
CHARLES SCRIBNER'S SONS
1923

COPYRIGHT, 1917, BY
CHARLES SCRIBNER'S SONS

Printed in the United States of America

Published September, 1917

TO

MY MOTHER

TO
MY MOTHER

PREFACE

ANY vital discussion of personal evangelism ought to be carried on between two individuals alone, if it is to be personal; and therein lies the difficulty in writing a book on this subject. We are natually reticent about our inner life and shrink instinctively from revealing those processes by which our spirits have been disciplined and made fit for true fellowship with God. Nevertheless, we who are Christians need to help people to understand the laws of cause and effect as they apply to Christian experience; we must be able to answer some of the practical questions that are put to us by those who seek reality in the spiritual life and need working principles; and we want, by our counsel, to help and not to hinder those who are within our influence. People do not usually find their way into the kingdom without some personal help. Our Lord spent a large portion of His time in dealing with the personal life of individuals and yet His chosen method has long been neglected by His followers.

This little book has been written in the hope that it may help to define the human element in the making of a Christian. It does not pretend to deal with that part of the Christian life which is hidden with Christ in God, but is concerned chiefly with the human side of Christian experience, the moral situation we have to face in our own hearts, and the personal challenge that we meet in the teachings of Jesus Christ. It is written in the belief that if we have a rational understanding of human nature and its normal reactions we can apply the message of the gospel with more wisdom and help many bewildered or discouraged people to find their heavenly Father.

Each chapter is arranged in two parts: a general discussion of the subject and a Bible study. The studies can be used for group or class discussions by leaders in Sunday-schools and Christian associations or by college students. The "References for Reading" in the Appendix will furnish supplemental material for the use of group leaders.

The writer is keenly conscious of her limitations in attempting to interpret the significance of a Christian life; but there are too many unshepherded folk in this time of world distress, and any bit of experience that might help one of the least of them must not be withheld.

B. C.

NEW YORK CITY,
July 31, 1917.

CONTENTS

THE CHALLENGE TO SERVICE

CHAPTER		PAGE
I.	Socializing My Faith	1
II.	Motives That Test	12
III.	Some Essential Convictions	19
IV.	Preparation for Service	28

GUIDING PRINCIPLES

V.	Some Laws That Condition Mental Reactions	36
VI.	The Development of a Normal Christian Experience	45
VII.	The Oneness of Spirit, Mind, and Body	53
VIII.	Requisite Conditions for Spiritual Comradeship	60
IX.	Releasing Spiritual Energy	68

THE APPLICATION OF THESE PRINCIPLES TO TYPES OF RELIGIOUS EXPERIENCE

X.	The Problem of the Nominal Christian	75
XI.	The Approach to the Non-Christian	85
XII.	The Approach to Those Who Have Intellectual Difficulties	94
XIII.	The Approach to Those Who Are Fighting Besetting Sins	105

CONTENTS

CHAPTER		PAGE
XIV.	The Approach to Those Who Face Problems of Conduct	115
XV.	The Approach to Those Who Live an Unbalanced Life	126
XVI.	The Approach to Those Who Are Feeling After Reality	132
XVII.	Developing the Religious Life of Children	138
XVIII.	The Sources of Growth	146
XIX.	The Perils of Success	152
	References for Reading	159

THE HUMAN ELEMENT IN
THE MAKING OF A CHRISTIAN

THE HUMAN ELEMENT IN THE MAKING OF A CHRISTIAN

CHAPTER I

SOCIALIZING MY FAITH

"The one thing of which I am sure these days," said a thoughtful man, "is that I am not sure of anything. I want something real, something that will show this mad world how to get a grip on something solid." "How about God?" asked his friend. "He is real to some of us." "Well, if He is, why don't all of you begin to make Him real to the rest of us? He can't be very real to most Christians or they wouldn't succeed so well in keeping Him out of all their conversation. If any one has help, this is the time of all times to give it." The ring of this challenge might well drive us to self-examination. It brings forth in sharp outline the contrast between our usual attitude toward the inarticulate longings of people and that of Jesus Christ. His intense interest in their spiritual needs is so unlike the dull apathy that most Christians show. How can we be sure that we *are* Christians when we are so far from possessing His spirit toward others? For "when He saw the multitudes, He was moved with compassion for them, because they were distressed and scattered, as sheep not having a shepherd. Then saith He unto His disciples, 'The harvest indeed is plenteous, but the laborers are few. Pray ye therefore the Lord of the harvest, that he send forth laborers into his harvest'" (Matt. 9 : 37, 38).

The harvest is even whiter now. The fact that three-fourths of the civilized world are in deadly combat after nineteen centuries of Christian teaching has filled our minds with questions and upset our theories. We Christians, though dazed, feel that some reply must be made to those who are saying quite frankly, "What is Christianity worth?" "Where is thy God?" for one hears this on all sides. The world is ready to talk about Him as never before.

We are faced, too, by frank questions about our social relationships. The world is becoming quite sure that the existing community conditions and their inherent injustices are obstacles that must and can be removed so that people if they want to can know God. The Christian conscience is becoming sensitive to social needs and is exacting a higher standard for a Christian life. People are hoping that some one will tell them how to use this social spirit in the creation of a social programme that will build up the kingdom of Jesus Christ on sure foundations. They are sure that He is related to it all in some way and they are ready to have His help and talk over His programme with any one who sees it from His point of view. We say to ourselves that it is chiefly a matter of education; that people need to be taught the ethical principles of Jesus Christ and the laws of social adjustment, and that a well-ordered community life based on justice and co-operation will solve our problems. Well, education is certainly doing a great deal and pointing the way so clearly that people are forced to own to their sins of omission. We see illustrations of this all about us. Recently a prominent manufacturer who had exploited the labor of children to swell his profits and had been for years the devout and respected church leader in his town and its philanthropies suddenly lost his religious influence in the community when people began to learn their social responsibility toward all little ones and began to apply the standards of Jesus Christ to the situation. The light of publicity is being thrown on unsanitary housing, sweat-shop conditions, and other social evils, and those who are responsible for them are either correcting them or concealing their connection with them.

We can plead ignorance no longer and we are face to face with a need for such moral decision of character as will purge us from our social sin. Responsibility is being located in the human will, and if we fail there we are in open disobedience to the light. The real social problem that we Christians have to face is found in the age-long fact that people know the good and do it not. Why is this so? Why does a man drink when he knows it ruins him? Why does a girl take coffee at ten o'clock at night when she knows she will lose a night's sleep? Why does a man allow foul drains to exist in a house he owns when he knows that the little children living there may die of typhoid? There are some, also, who see the beauty of a Christian life of fellowship with God and yet are unwilling to pay the price in order to have it themselves.

That was a revealing sentence in the leading address at a conference of social workers: "After the minimum-wage law has been passed, after the child-labor laws have been enacted, there yet remain the souls of people." It is a quiet admission that more than law is needful; the inner desires and choices of people's hearts must direct the will toward the enforcement of the law. It is the lesson of the Old Testament which the prophets discerned. The laws of God must be written in the hearts of people before they will become effective. Yes, indeed, all our social justice for which we ought to fight is only one part of the work; "there yet remain the souls of people" who know the good and do it not, who must be touched not alone by the precise counsels of education but who must catch the contagion of Christian character from association with those whose "character," as John Stuart Mill says, "is a perfectly fashioned will," one which does always those things that please God.

It is a big task that we have been given, with two distinct parts: to turn the calcium-light of God's righteousness upon all the conditions of our day until people see what He wants, and see too, how miserably far short of His expectation we have come in doing what we want at the expense of others; then to lead people to want and to will what God wants and wills by drawing near to them in love and sharing with them our relationship with Him until they cannot resist the appeal of His love. When this is done we must then link ourselves with all who will to apply our united will to the bringing in of God's kingdom.

This kind of work cannot be done through books or laws alone, any more than a little child can be educated apart from association with personalities that have had more experience with life and its meanings. It must be by example, or, as the small boy once put it: "Our teacher teaches us boys to be polite." "How does she do it?" asked his mother. "Oh, I don't know. She just walks around—and we feel as polite as anything." Thus it is that our great gift to our generation is that we be what we ought to be and bring others in touch with the source of our life and victory.

We know that the chief source of our life is the reality of God as we come to know Him in Jesus Christ, who gives us the power to be and to do what we ought to be and to do. We know that all society needs this power to create new desires in the heart and give a new moral drive to the will. This can only be achieved when we begin to socialize our faith and to share it; for multitudes of people will never come to know God unless they find Him with our personal help. Many of them question the efficiency of the church because the social upheavals have seemed to contradict her voice. They do not know where to turn for help if we who rub elbows with them in the jostle of business and social life are silent. We dare not fail them when the meaning of the word Christian is being redefined by common consent with a new accent on social relationships. This voice of the people calls attention to our daily living and invites a close scrutiny. The gospel of a life is the only Bible many people will ever read. The masses of people are more influenced in their attitude toward God as He is seen through the ordinary manifestations of Christianity by the spirit and walk of us who are their friends than by any other means. Of course if we have no conscious ideals of the Christian life that are worth sharing, they will soon find us out; but if we really have them they will want them, and we would be unworthy, indeed, if we were smugly selfish about them. We have our great opportunity to give our best, sure that some wistful-eyed folk will turn to us to listen.

Surely some very human prophets are needed to-day; some who can give voice to the stifled convictions of people and interpret them in the light of the true character of God, Who is adequate for all that the human heart and society craves. As we try to think it through there are four elemental needs in human life to-day:

(1) *The need of a vision.* "Where there is no vision," the proverb runs, "the people perish." It is all too true. We live and grow by our visions; dreams, that call out our pluck and will to make them real. A girl dreams of herself as a college woman, and she buckles down to her elementary studies with a vim that makes the dream come true. A man dreams of a

little home with wife and children, and he plods along in his business and makes of himself a man worthy to support a home. The girl has her vision because she has seen a college girl the personification of her ideal; the man has seen a home and the ideal lures him on. The latent powers of each are called out by the concrete vision. So it is with the spiritual life. People "feel," as the poet says, "a Presence that disturbs" and they have all sorts of ideas about God. They may know the historical facts of the life of Jesus Christ or they may not. At any rate, if they do know about Him, it is as a dim tale of some one who because He walked the earth long ago is totally unrelated to the twentieth century. They need a vision of Him now in this day that is only possible when God is allowed to live in us by His Spirit and use us as the embodiment of His truth and love until people see Him incarnate in terms of human life that they can understand. In other words, God must become personal to them. The church and her religious teaching seem so impersonal to the multitudes; they need to be mediated to them through the life of some person. "I would give anything I possess to have a faith in God like yours," said a long-time unbeliever to a Christian friend. "I've always known what the Bible says about it, but I never saw any one before who had the nerve to live it. You've given my thinking a jolt." People to-day need many jolts like that; if they see the vision of God in a life they will find it hard to resist.

(2) *The need for sympathy and companionship in suffering and the restoration of the life marred by mistakes.* One of the big burdens that people carry is the load of loneliness that becomes too bitter to be borne when the fact of sorrow and suffering presses close. To suffer and to be alone in it with no understanding friend near by brings despair. What a poor appeal we could make to most people in the world to-day if we could not bring to them a living Lord who is "touched with the feeling of our infirmities" and who shares our sufferings. The value of suffering is one of the big mysteries of life; but it is an unescapable fact which does not cease to be even though we ignore it or deny it or run away from it. Without it some of the richest gifts of experience and character are lost. Chief among these is the sense of God's intimate understanding that humbles us with wonder that He should care about all we feel, suffer with us, and give His strength and help. There are

thousands about us who have not this comfort. They are haunted by the cry of their hearts:

> "What can it mean? Is it aught to Him
> That the nights are long and the days are dim?
> Can He be touched by the griefs I bear,
> Which sadden the heart and whiten the hair?
> Around His throne are eternal calms,
> And strong glad music of happy psalms,
> And bliss unruffled by any strife;
> How can He care for my little life?

> "When shadows hang o'er me the whole day long,
> And my spirit is bowed with shame and wrong;
> When I am not good and the deeper shade
> Of conscious sin makes my heart afraid,
> And the busy world has too much to do
> To stay in its course to help me through,
> And I long for a Saviour,—can it be
> That the God of the universe cares for me?"

The wonderful truth that God as we see Him in Jesus Christ identifies himself with the struggle and pain of this world is what people need to see more clearly. They need the comfort and courage that comes from the realization that they do not walk alone, bearing the brunt of the consequences of their mortality, but that God himself is under the burden. Now, how shall people see this and find their understanding Father unless those who live in His Spirit get under the burdens of people with love and sympathy and courage. "Hereby perceive we the love of God, because he laid down his life for us: and we ought to lay down our lives for the brethren" (I John 3 : 16).

It is not a system of ethics that people need so much as an understanding friend through whom they come to know the very heart of God. We need to confess our sin of pride and fastidiousness that has made us shun the pain of others and shirk our duty to give our strength to their weakness. People will never come to know their heavenly Father until they see Him walking the streets in the temple of our bodies, ministering to those sick, and in prison, and naked and hungry. Has our Christian life ever cost us inconvenience, suffering, and sacrifice for others? How far are we willing to enter vicariously into the "fellowship of His sufferings"?

> "Lead me, yea, lead me deeper into life,
> This suffering, human life wherein Thou liv'st
> And breathest still, and holdst thy way divine.
> 'Tis here, O pitying Christ, where thee I seek,
> Here where the strife is fiercest; where the sun
> Beats down upon the highway thronged with men,
> And in the raging mart, O! deeper lead
> My soul into the living world of souls
> Where Thou dost move."
>
> *(Richard Watson Gilder.)*

But it is not only help in pain that people need in order to see the Father but the restoration of fellowship with Him as their Redeemer from sin. If there were no way in which God could restore the spirit of people who suffer because of their sin or the sin of others, and heal the open sore that blights humanity, all our efforts at social reform would be futile. Back of every social problem lies the fact of sin and the active energy of sin; back of all unbrotherliness there is sin. It is the age-long, ugly fact with which we have to reckon. What good will it do to keep cleaning the basin of the fountain so long as the filth comes pouring out from the waters. We must get at the source and find our true help. In other words, the continuous attitude of the loving God, which was once revealed in the historic fact of Jesus Christ on His cross, must be so brought home to the hearts of people that they will hate sin as He hated it. As He refrained from no cost to cure it, so those who sin will find His healing and be restored to a friendship with God, forgiven and cleansed. People can read rules of ethics and be taught ideals but they can only see and receive the truth of the cross of Christ as it is ministered to them through those of us who carry the marks of the Lord Jesus in humble hearts and can speak out of a full experience to those who need a Redeemer. And from the streams of living water that flow out from a cleansed heart the mire and filth of this world will be washed away. If we were finding honestly, for ourselves, the restoring power of God by letting Him deal with our sin we would find some of the same spirit burning in us that set Paul on fire whom Myers so truly depicts in his lines:

> "Oft when the Word is on me to deliver
> Lifts the illusion and the truth lies bare,
> Desert or mountain, the city or the river
> Melts in a lucid paradise of air.

Only like souls I see the folk thereunder
Bound who should conquer, slaves who should be kings,
Hearing their one hope with an empty wonder,
Sadly contented with the show of things.
Then with a rush the intolerable craving
Shivers throughout me like a trumpet call,
Oh, to save these! to perish for their saving!
Die for their life, be offered for them all!"

(3) *The need for a love that will make the dream of brotherhood a tangible reality.* We all talk about the love of God and yet take pride in being most exclusive in our love toward others. We look at it so often as a personal luxury to be used only when a fortuitous combination of circumstances proves irresistible. We are so satisfied with a few understanding spirits and fail utterly to appreciate multitudes of others because we are blind and stupid and only half-awake. Professor William James speaks of the "great cloud-bank of ancestral blindness weighing down upon us, only transiently riven here and there by fitful revelations of the truth"; and he shows how this blindness keeps us from discerning the possibility of the ideal life in other people. It is all true. Most of us are so limited in our insight into the true nature of others that we go on through life appreciating only a few of the personalities we meet. Indeed, we are so blind to the inner life of people that we often are surprised to discover that certain persons should have any friends at all, and say to ourselves: "I cannot see what any one can find to satisfy himself in that individual." It is our blindness and stupidity that keeps us from realizing people as they are, and it is fortunate, indeed, for us all that there are some friends keener than we are who respond to us and appreciate what is hidden in us. There are certain people who have a great capacity for friendship, merely because they are open-eyed enough to see the beauty of personality and to delight in it. Such people get the most out of life.

Love never hurts any one and it is God's own medium for understanding Him and bringing others nearer to Him. The bonds of brotherhood are real when people are bound together by common experiences and trials, but they never are severed if they are knit together by love. Love not only helps us to realize the inner ideal and dignity of all other people but is the active creative force that calls out latent powers and transforms discord into harmony. The more the vision of God in Jesus Christ holds the attention and the more real becomes the sense of God's forgiveness and friendship, the easier will it be to look at others with the active spirit of love instead of stodgy indifference. In this way we gain stature in personality and find our largest life and call out others also into fulness of life.

The ideal of Christian brotherhood which Jesus Christ holds up is nothing short of the perfect bond. "And this is my commandment that ye love one another, as *I have loved you.*" Are we willing to socialize not only our faith but our love to this extent?

(4) *The need for some moral dynamic in order that social ideals may be worked out.* We have not been slow about sharing our social ideals. We have socialized our working laws of hygiene, we have socialized our ideals for the relation of capital and labor, for recreation and education, suffrage and social morality. But in it all we have kept to ourselves the only thing that will make any of these ideals personal and potent. We have not socialized our faith in our living God revealed through Jesus Christ. We have researched the valley of dry bones, like the prophet of old, and brought together through the ordered ways of social laws and organizations bone to bone until out of the chaotic mass a mighty army for social betterment takes shape. We have done all that human wisdom can do, but the army is still inert; it needs the breath of God that it may arise and live and do. If only we could make the connection between sharing our faith and sharing our ideals! It is here that we Christians fail so pitifully. Some of us go out armed with ideals, some of us with faith. We all fail because we are not completely furnished. Those who preach social ideals fail to give a permanent motive power to the will, which alone can come from a vital Christian faith; those who preach faith often lack the laboratory work that would show people the application of the ideal. If only God would open our eyes to see our need until we should see the whole truth! All that we have done is right, but we must not leave the other undone. Let us socialize our ideals and socialize our working faith in God until we shall not need to say: "Know Jehovah, for they shall all know me, from the least of them unto the greatest of them, saith Jehovah" (Jer. 31 : 34).

BIBLE STUDY I

SHARING OUR CHRISTIAN CONVICTIONS.—A NATURAL SERVICE

I. *The interdependence of our individual life and the life of society.*

Read Isaiah 58 : 1–12. Note in detail the marks of formalism and self-centredness in the verses 2–4—a reluctant conforming to some supposed requirement of God for which they expect merit and reward; not a co-operation with His purposes for His children. Verses 6–11. Write down the programme of service that God desires carried out. In what ways would it involve us in a living sacrifice? Note the force of the word *"Then"* in verse 8 and verse 10. What are the spiritual rewards promised in verses 8–11? Is there any inherent reason why these rewards cannot be ours apart from society? How is our own human destiny dependent on our earning these rewards?

II. *Sharing our convictions—an inevitable service for every true Christian.*

Read Acts 4 : 18–20. The heart naturally expresses what it really experiences. In view of this, what is the natural inference when we are silent? Some Bible illustrations of this law:
  (1) *Water.*—John 7 : 37, 38. How does a river differ from a pool? What is the result when we dam a river?
  (2) *Fire.*—Luke 11 : 33. Note the significance of the words "That *they* which enter in *may see* the light." What happens to a light when it is hidden under a bushel? How does the experience of Jeremiah confirm this? See Jer. 20 : 9.
  (3) *Branch.*—John 15 : 5. Consider the solemn warning of our Lord in verse 6—the penalty of a fruitless life.
  (4) *Friendship.*—John 15 : 27. What are the obligations of friendship? Why do we depend upon our friends to interpret us to others? I John 3 : 16, 17. A friend in need compels love and sacrifice. Laying down our life is often letting our life be where we do not want it to be.

In the light of these illustrations read Matt. 12 : 34.

III. *The gospel of Jesus Christ—a social gospel.*

Read I John 1 : 3 as a statement of the objective of the spiritual revelation—the "noblesse oblige" of the gospel.

Read John 17 : 19. What are the strongest motives that lead us to seek personal regeneration?

If "character is caught and not taught," what is the importance of Paul's advice to Timothy in I Tim. 4 : 12, 15, 16? How many of the virtues in verse 12 are social in their implication? Verse 14. Each has his own gift; we are not asked to do what some one with other gifts has done, but to use the gift that is in us.

Read Psalm 67. What motives does the Psalmist urge as a reason why God should give a personal blessing?

Whether we do it consciously or not, we *are* interpreting our conception of God to one another each day, through the many relationships we have in business and society, making it easier or more difficult for each of us to realize our heavenly Father. We cannot detach the spiritual from the human or the individual from the group. Is there any one in the group of those who minister to my life who finds it harder to love God because of me? See Matt. 23 : 13. In what concrete ways do we hinder those who are trying to enter into the kingdom?

"We must be here to work;
And men who work, can only work for men,
And, not to work in vain, must comprehend
Humanity, and, so, work humanly,
And raise men's bodies still by raising souls,
As God did, first.

"'But stand upon the earth,'
I said, 'to raise them—(this is human, too;
There's nothing high which has not first been low;
My humbleness, said One, has made Me great!)
As God did, last.'

"'And work all silently,
And simply,' he returned, 'as God does all;
Distort our nature never, for our work,
Nor count our right hands stronger for being hoofs.
The man most man, with tenderest human hands,
Works best for men,—as God in Nazareth.'"

(*Mrs. E. B. Browning.*)

CHAPTER II

MOTIVES THAT TEST

Most of us find it easy to say "yes" with our minds to the need for socializing our faith, but we are reluctant to focus our powers upon this as our supreme personal privilege. There may lurk in our minds the question as old as time, "Am I my brother's keeper?" or, to put it more explicitly, "Am I responsible for what my friend thinks concerning God and Christ and life?" Our imagination needs to be filled by something that will supply motive power to our wills and start us on our task. It is well, therefore, to face some of the facts about ourselves that should lead us to begin to share our gift of life with others. The following motives have sufficed to start others; do they suffice for you?

A fine sense of honor in discharging the great debt we owe to others who in the past have been faithful to our personal need. How can we repay our Christian forebears, the church, our mothers and fathers and friends? By them our hearts were kept tender toward God and from them came the sources of our knowledge of Him and of our strength of character. The light that came to us in our spiritual struggles was born of the sympathetic love of God, usually voiced by some Christian friend. We can only repay the debt by thinking of it as a loan to be passed on to others who need the same help. How could we have met the crises of our lives without this help from others! Our real gratitude is measured by the way we share our greatest gift!

The reasonable expectation of those who are in spiritual fog and darkness and who know that we have had experience in finding the way. It is a serious matter to fail a friend in need. A Christian student in an eastern college had as a close friend a girl from a non-Christian home. In all their friendly conversations during four years no word was spoken concerning God and the personal relationship to Christ. Three years after graduation, in reply to a letter written out of sympathy for the loss of her mother, the non-Christian friend said: "Why didn't you tell me about the possibility of knowing God before? I used to long to have you speak to me when at college, but I did not open my heart, for it was so dark and full of fear. I thought your attitude toward God must be temperamental and not for me else surely you would have helped me to find Him. You know how hard my life has been. Why didn't you tell me this before?" It is not unlikely that some one near us, whom we least suspect, is thinking similar thoughts about us.

> "Last night, oh, friend of mine, unto your door
> With wearied soul and heart most sore
> I came to cry your comforting—and you
> Gave me light words, light praise, your jester's due;
> I shall not come for comfort any more.
>
> "Take you my laughter since you love it so—
> The little jests men juggle to and fro;
> I did not guess how much I came to ask
> Your solace for a heart you do not know."
> *(Theodosia Garrison.)*

The preservation of one's own spiritual life which demands action and expression. The blessings of God stream into our life from countless channels. We are the terminal, and a terminal is temporarily a storehouse that it may be constantly a distributing centre. We are so made that we cannot live even our own inner life to ourselves. It is only real as it is shared and expressed in action. If we try to hug to ourselves our inner desires and impulses we soon cease to have them. They die because they are unsatisfied. If a light is hidden under a bushel it either burns up the bushel or goes out. If we are moved by the spirit of love we must find some one to love or we lose it. Love is impossible without a relationship. It is a social force. It was inevitable that a God of love should give His Son to express His heart in terms that we could understand; in like manner we, too, love only as we give expression to it. Perhaps some of us are suffering from spiritual atrophy just because we have succeeded so well in restraining all healthy expression of our Christian life. We need to fear lest we lose our gift of life just because we hide it away as did the man in the parable who had his talent taken away from him.

The potential value of one life when controlled by Christ. Those of us who have the teacher instinct are more likely to be moved by this thought than others. No one can estimate the power of a single life when all its energies are released for the kingdom of God. One has only to recall the biographies of men like David Livingstone, Chinese Gordon, Phillips Brooks, Florence Nightingale, Madame Guyon, Isabella Thoburn, D. L. Moody, and college men like Forbes Robinson, Hugh Beaver, and Horace Rose, as well as countless living examples, to realize how important one redeemed life may be for the far-reaching purposes of God. Possibly a larger proportion of potential leadership is to be found in the colleges of the world than elsewhere. If so, the winning of a student to a Christ-controlled life should be of compelling importance.

We never know whom we are touching, and the most insignificant boy or girl may play an important part in the world's service. It may be that an incidental touch that we may have with that life in the name of Christ will be the most important part of our life's work. Therefore we may well take heed that we do not miss our opportunity, through lack of readiness to help, in releasing the spiritual possibilities of even one life.

The command of Christ and its unmistakable appeal to loyal disciples. The Christian has pledged obedience to the will of God and the will of God is expressed in the purpose of Christ: "I am come that they may have life, and may have it abundantly" (John 10 : 10). The application of this purpose to the friends of Christ is made very plain in His words spoken after His resurrection: "Peace be unto you: as the Father hath sent me even so send I you." If those humble fisherfolk had gone back to their fishing and had not taken this command of Christ literally, we, like our ancestors, might yet have been dancing round Druid altars. Fortunate it is for us that Christ's faith in the faithfulness of His friends was not disappointed, but that they did just as He told them and began to share the knowledge of Him with friends and foes alike; for we are the inheritors of all the blessings and knowledge. The same commands are as binding on us as they were on the first friends of Christ, and we, too, can only show our love and loyalty to Him by obeying them. This ought to supply sufficient motive for a life of service.

The spirit of ambition and the love of conquest. There is something in each one of us that longs to achieve, to overcome, to subdue. The "fighting quality" in our natures is God-given, and without it progress is impossible. Multitudes of people fight for money, fame, or social position, counting no sacrifice too great. This energy of ambition saps the strength and peace of mind of a person merely because it is directed to ends that are selfish and material. If the same force were directed toward the bringing in of the kingdom of our Lord in this world and in the hearts of people it would be a great tonic and would call into play all our latent powers. Professor James suggests that this world needs more than anything else "the moral equivalent of war." Could this not be found if we should fix our ambitions on the lifelong war that must be waged for character in ourselves and in others who need our help?

> "No, when the fight begins within himself,
> A man's worth something, God stoops o'er his hand,
> Satan looks up between his feet,—both tug—
> He's left, himself, i' the middle: the soul awakes
> And grows. Prolong that battle through this life!
> Never leave growing till the life to come."
> (*Robert Browning*.)

The need of the Christless world. This need cannot be fully realized by us because it has never been a fact of our experience. Many Christians can recall the intense hunger, loneliness, and despair of the days when they were seeking a living Saviour and friend. But the students of the Occident cannot appreciate the state of a people who have no hunger because they have not had food; whose loneliness is all the more bitter because they have never been lightened by hope. Now and then we are given a glimpse into a heart that should call forth our compassion and compel our help. Some years ago the *Baltimore Sun* published a letter written December, 1890, by a well-known senator to his wife. In it he writes as follows: "What an uncivil host life is, to invite us to an entertainment which we are compelled to attend whether we like it or not, and then unceremoniously to take us by the arm and bow us out into the night, stormy and dismal, to go stumbling about without so much as a lantern to show us the way to another town—" When one realizes that darkness and uncertainty abide in every heart that has no living relationship with Christ, the common bond of humanity should compel one to make any sacrifice of time and effort to relate a life to the Christ who said: "I am the light of the world; he that followeth Me shall not walk in darkness but shall have the light of life" (John 8 : 12).

Doctor A. J. Gordon once said: "I used to pray often, 'Lord, have compassion on a lost world.' At last He said to me: 'I have had compassion; it is now for you to have compassion— I gave my heart, give yours.'"

The expectant love of Christ. This motive will make its strongest appeal to those who are in sincere and sympathetic partnership with Christ in redeeming lives. The strength of the appeal is measured by one's fidelity to the life of friendship with Christ. One dare not fail the expectant love of such a friend. The sweetness of all communion with God is conditioned by the depth of our appreciation of the great purposes of His heart and the work in which He is most deeply interested. Surely that is centred around the eternal good of His children over whom He watches constantly and to whom He speaks through other children who have caught a little more of His spirit and who have the strength, if they will use it, to help His little ones to know Him better. It is in our power to release or restrain the life-giving voice of God in this world. If we want to hear it for ourselves we can scarcely dare to deprive any other child who will hear it best only when voiced through us.

The contagious spirit of joy. People were meant to have joy in life. God has done His part in providing a world of beauty, in creating the infinite variety of human personalities, and in giving us all a capacity for living joyously; and yet in spite of God's purpose for His children there is unhappiness and discontent everywhere. This is the tragedy of life. Of course, we may shut our eyes to it and refuse to see or think of anything that is not joyous and beautiful, but we cannot get close to many people and share their life without facing the fact of sorrow and pain. Most of the sharpness of it comes from a sense of loneliness and misunderstanding. If people could only see their loving heavenly Father guiding, sympathizing, and loving them, a deep joy would enter in that would of itself be a great healing force. Some of us love people so well that we want them to have joy and gladness of heart—a joy that circumstances cannot alter. We have this gift of joy in our hands because we know our Father and are sure of His love, and we can reassure others of His love for them and restore their joy. There is no joy in life like bringing joy to others. We all want it above all things, therefore no price is too great to pay for it —especially when it is what God desires for His children.

BIBLE STUDY II
The Claim of Christ's Call

I. *The claim of simple loyalty to the personal relation we have with Christ.*

See Matt. 10 : 32. Every true relationship is dependent on loyalty. This teaching is not an arbitrary statement but the inevitable situation that exists in every true relationship. If one friend is loyal and the other is not, *can* there be any real relationship? In the light of this, what is our obligation to confess our loyalty to Christ?

Read Phil. 1 : 20. What is the usual cause of our disloyalty to our relationship with Christ? What did it cost our Lord to be loyal to us? Can we accept the natural inference of Matt. 10 : 24, 25?

II. *The claim of the kingdom which can only be set up with the co-operation of the citizens of the kingdom.*

Read Matt. 28 : 19, 20. On what does the promise of Christ's presence depend? Why is it that our personal sense of His power and presence is conditioned by the claims of His kingdom?

III. *The claim of Christ's ambition that we should share His glory.*

Read John 17 : 18 and John 20 : 21. What is the measure of the "even so"? How does that challenge our wills? What concrete service does it involve? See John 15 : 16, 17. Jesus Christ chose us to do His work and we are not presumptuous when we undertake to do it. When we begin to obey this call we transform our ideal of life from a series of unrelated acts to a continuous purpose where "all things work together for good" and abide even unto eternity.

IV. *The challenge of Christ's example.*

See Matt. 9 : 36–38. What do we usually see in a multitude? How is a spirit of compassion developed in any one? How does the teaching of verse 38 take for granted that we, too, will have the same spirit and sense of responsibility that Jesus had?

See Matt. 10 : 24, 25 and John 13 : 14–17. What are the inferences if we do not accept these challenges? Identification of life with our Lord always implies identification of purpose and work.

V. *The claim of a possible task—even humanly possible—therefore we are without excuse.*

Read Matt. 25 and Matt. 10 : 42. How may we give personal service to Christ now? Why are the righteous surprised (verse 37) at the words of Christ in verses 35 and 36? It is possible for every one to do as unto God the countless acts of service to our fellow men. Every relationship thus becomes a sacrament—a symbol of our desires toward God.

If all these challenges are reasonable then we need to heed Rev. 22 : 17 as the will of God for us: "He that heareth, let him say *Come!*"

> "The night lies dark upon the earth, and we have light,
> So many grope their way, and we have sight.
> One faith is theirs and ours, of sin and care,
> But we are borne along, while they their burden bear.
> Footsore, heart-weary, faint they on the way,
> Mute in their sorrow, while we kneel and pray.
>
> . . . .
>
> Father, why is it that these millions roam,
> And guess that that is Home, and urge their way.
> Is it enough to keep the door ajar that they may come and pray?"

CHAPTER III

SOME ESSENTIAL CONVICTIONS

If the case has been made clear in the preceding chapters, and we are morally honest, we have come to the point where we are awake to our duty and want to do it. We may feel as helpless as children but we do not mean to shirk. We want to begin to think straight and to learn how to do our duty.

We ourselves need transformation before we can help others. Certain elemental truths must begin to work anew in our hearts and be real to us. In writing to the Romans Paul says: "*Be transformed by the entire renewal of your minds*, so that you may learn by experience what God's will is, that will which is good and beautiful and perfect" (Romans 12 : 2, Weymouth translation), and he here tells us the secret. Our transformation depends on certain convictions of mind which give us courage to face our task and lead us out into God's will. Some of these convictions are already axioms in our experience, but have ceased to hold our attention because they are taken for granted. Let us look at some of these attitudes of mind, for we must hold to them steadily if we are naturally to find ourselves in the midst of opportunities for service. We may well let our imagination take hold of them until we are under the spell of them and shape our conduct by them.

The first of these is the fact that God is infinitely eager to get points of contact with the hearts of His children. He is waiting to illumine the heart that will open to Him with even more certainty than is the summer sun to flood a room with light when the curtains are raised. Now there are many of us who do not really believe this; if we did, we would be more eager to help uplift the curtains from sordid or blind hearts. We are more likely to wonder why God allows so many to live in darkness rather than to wonder why, when the sun is shining, we should be so stupid as not to knock at other people's doors and tell them to lift up the curtains.

> "Ah, what a web
> Of gray inconsequential-seeming threads!
> The modish thoughts, the meat and money thoughts—
> In webs, in webs, in iron curtains proof
> Against whatever fires of poesy
> Burn in white aspirations from our lives,
> They hang between us and your inner eyes,
> Those better eyes, the pure eyes of the soul.
>
> "Lift up the curtain: For an hour lift up
> The veil that holds you prisoners in this world
> Of coins and wines and motor-horns, this world
> Of figures and of men who trust in facts
> This pitiable, hypocritic world
> Where men with blinkered eyes and hobbled feet
> Grope down a narrow gorge and call it life."
>   (*The Heart of Youth*, Herman Hagedorn.)

In other words, our task is to remind people of the sunshine and persuade them to open the windows—the sunshine does the rest. Our share is incidental. God will make Himself plain if once He gets access to a heart. We can count upon Him and His work; we only prepare the way for Him. It is the truth that is burning in the heart of our Lord when He says of His blind people: "How oft would I have gathered thee as a hen gathereth her chickens under her wings, but ye would not." Oh, that we would feel the pathos of this enough to want to persuade the blinded, foolish people of to-day to come to Him!

Another attitude of mind that we need is one of expectancy and alertness. We are so short-sighted in our vision and can see such a little way into the future that most of life comes to us full of unexpected happenings and experiences. We do believe that God is eager to get into the heart of every child of His and that He is behind all the changing scenes of life; but this implies that we ought to count upon the fact that no living beings are ever stationary but that they change ever, from bad to worse or from good to better. Therefore we cannot speak of any one as hopeless, for perhaps there may have been some experience yesterday which changed the whole point of view and which will make that unresponsive soul responsive to-day. We generally get what we are looking for, and if we are expecting that our Lord will gain access to the heart of a friend, we at least shall be ready to hear the sound of

His footsteps and prepare the way for His coming. We need to train ourselves in that aspect of faith to have, as Father Bull counsels, "that buoyant expectation of the improbable which refuses the dull estimates of common sense and joyfully expects in the future what is not suggested by the experience of the past." And he adds: "When there is a childlike expectation of the improbable, there will be the manifestation of God's saving power." This daily conviction will forever prevent our taking that Morris-chair attitude toward our friends, in which we sit back and look at life as an entertaining spectacle. We shall be on tiptoe eager to see in what new ways God will manifest Himself to people and how we can help them to see Him. "Therefore be ye also ready: for in an hour that ye think not the Son of Man cometh" (Matt. 24 : 44).

Again, our experience in life ought to teach us the value of the incidental; we shall then have a greater reverence for little happenings. We all believe that God is back of this world of events; that, as Jesus said, "not a sparrow falls to the ground without your Father"—that nothing happens by chance or accident. Therefore, we never know when our most important opportunity may come. The testimony of many people goes to show that some incidental meeting with a friend, when a simple question was asked or some unconscious loyalty to God was shown, has marked the turning-point in a life. That obscure disciple, Andrew, little suspected when he brought Peter to see Jesus that he was doing his greatest life-work that day, for how could he have foreseen the day when this same Peter would bring five thousand to bow before his Lord through one sermon? Andrew never brought people to God by multitudes directly, but his life service was just as wonderful because he brought to Jesus the man who brought the multitudes.

God only knows how many chances for great service come to us in disguise and are lost because we were looking for something we thought truly great. A Christian girl at a summer hotel gathered three noisy children about her one Sunday afternoon and told them Bible stories by the lake, closing with the story of Jesus by the Sea of Galilee. They were quiet but did not seem specially impressed. She had at least relieved the grown folk for an hour, she reflected. A week later a woman of wealth and social position wrote her a note and asked to see her. When they met she said: "I want to talk with you about God, for I know you know Him. My little nephew came to see me and told me about the wonderful stories you told him last Sunday. I am an unhappy woman and must find help somewhere." Help came and the woman was led to her Lord and to work for the kingdom of God. In the faithfulness to the noisy children came the great opportunity to bless multitudes. To all of us who are ready for service incidental opportunities will come, which in retrospect will be seen as little hinges on which some door swung into a new and undiscovered country.

The zest of adventure is ever near us if we have the right perspective and will lead us to be more faithful in that which is least in order that we may be trusted with that which is great. We should form the habit of asking ourselves constantly: "Why am I brought into touch with this person?" "What help am I to gain from this relationship, or what am I to give to it?" "Why, of all the people in the world, should this one have been brought near me to-day?" "What is my Father's purpose in it?" There is nothing that will so keep the keen zest for life alive in us as keeping these questions ever in mind and watching for the answers.

We need also to remind ourselves that we can only meet life with life. Personal service for others is not a bit of work that can be taken up or dropped as we please. It knows no time element. It must be an unvarying attitude of mind that brings the whole of one's life alongside of the whole need of another. It is often not the amount of precise counsel that will help, though that, too, may be necessary; it is rather the natural comradeship of a sincere and loyal friend who does not direct people to a distant point but who walks with them along the path showing the beauties of the way and helping them to avoid pitfalls. An impersonal precept may give us light and a certain amount of wisdom—a guide-post does this—but it does not win our devotion or compel our wills until it comes to us incarnated in the life of some one who walks along with us. We have believed the truth of this, or at least we have thought we did, but we need to believe it *so hard* that we shall not go among human beings like a tortoise, ever carrying a shell and retreating within our shells at the first approach. How should we ever have known God if there ever had been times in the life of Jesus Christ when He was not transparently open and accessible to people! It was all a part of the laying down of His life, and "He left us an example that we should follow in His steps."

It is necessary also that we really believe that the relation of the spirit to its God is a fundamental interest in the life of every human being. We might as well take it for granted that people *are* interested in the things of the spiritual life even though they are not willing yet to admit this fact to any one. This is often due not so much to secretiveness as to the fact that nothing that they have seen in our lives measures up to the inner standard which they believe to be Christian. Or they may not be appealed to by the way in which we express our interest in the religious life, or they may be outside the narrow conceptions which we ourselves may have of the word Christian. The world is full of people who are judged by Christians as non-Christian merely because they do not attach the same value to certain religious forms, or because they interpret the Scriptures differently from other people or emphasize a different set of virtues. There are those, too, who make no professions of faith and have never become open disciples of Jesus Christ because they honestly do not know the way and have never seen any one who cared enough about it, seemingly, to teach them, or they have been repelled because people assumed that they were not interested. "They all think I'm a thorough worldling here, therefore I don't want to disappoint them," a girl said gayly to a chance acquaintance. "I don't believe for one moment that you are," came the reply. "I'll warrant God is in your thoughts constantly." "You're right; He is," she said, "and sometimes I wish I knew how people come to know Him." The rest was simple. Because this stranger had taken it for granted that this girl, in common with all humanity, had a thirst for God she was able to bring her into a living relationship with Him through a sincere sharing of what she knew through her own experience. No matter how thick the shell of conventionality and other interests may be, underneath there is a real life that really cares about knowing God. It is only those who can discern those hidden qualities of the spirit that earn the right to enter and have fellowship in the name of Christ.

There is another axiom of the spiritual life that most of us have ceased to count upon except as a refuge in an emergency.

It is that God is able to work in us, that His power "creates within us the desire to do His gracious will and also brings about the accomplishment of the desire" (Phil. 2 : 13, Weymouth). The omnipotence of God seems rather a far-away fact than a present source of confidence. If we really believed that His power is available for the accomplishment of every holy desire, there would be no limit to what we might do in His name. We should then see that it is His power working in us that leads us to discern the heart of another who is feeling out to know Him, and we should recognize this as a sure sign that He would work in that life through us in response to intercession, and we should pray with all our hearts that if He had created in us this desire to help He would bring about its accomplishment in His own time and way. Then we would watch to see how it would come about, and we would find ourselves at last confronted by a natural opportunity to give the help we longed to give, and another life would find its Father through us. The trouble with us is that we do not recognize His work in us, creating desires and giving us power to discern our opportunities. If we were to begin to count upon this principle as an unvarying certainty, we would then begin to use the resources of prayer and have our eyes made alert to see our opportunity. We need not pray for more opportunities but for the eyes to *see* them as they lie about us. God easily establishes natural connections between ourselves and others who need us when we are ready to be used.

We also need to remember that the spiritual life does not grow through a conflict of human opinion about God and life, but by a conviction of heart that issues in a will to follow on in obedience. It is not necessary that any one of us should be able to answer satisfactorily all questions and explain all mysteries concerning God, but it is necessary that each of us should see something in the God revealed by Jesus Christ, that compels the love of our wills if not the love of our feelings and leads us to begin to obey Him and give over the control of our life. We thus meet the challenge of the words: "If any man willeth to do his will he shall know by the teaching whether I come from God or whether I speak from myself" (John 7 : 17). All the light of knowledge and experience takes new meaning as it is related to God as the centre of our orbit, and we grow in grace and in the knowledge of our Lord Jesus Christ by the same processes with which we learned in school to know the world of facts. The chief business then was to secure the right teacher, then everything came as a matter of course. Thus it is with our knowledge of God. What we need and others need is to find the great Master Teacher and relate ourselves and our friends to Him in trust and obedience; then He works through our minds and hearts and guides us into all the truth by His Holy Spirit.

The test comes just here. People are blind to God's Fatherhood through ignorance or neglect, or they are so taken up with their own little experiments that they are content to follow their own wills, or they shrink from the discipline of the school of life. They need to be persuaded and lured on by the joyous comradeship of all of us who have already begun to enter into the joy of our Lord. It is not difficult to win other disciples if we are willing to share our experiences. Some of us know even now many who are thirsting for something, they know not what; are we ready to share with them our spiritual life from this time on? Saint Augustine once prayed in his time of struggle, before he had settled forever that God should control his life: "O God, give me chastity—but not *now!*" Perhaps we too are praying: "O God, give me the chance to help others to know Thee—but I'm not ready now!" If so, we might well not go on any farther until we can ask with all our heart: "O God, give me the chance to help others to know Thee—and I am ready now!"

BIBLE STUDY III

A Picture of the Heart of God

I. *The seeking God.*

Read Ezek. 34 : 1–16. What is the conception of God as pictured by the prophet? How does His attitude toward the sheep differ from that of the shepherds of Israel? Describe the kinds of experiences the sheep were having which moved the heart of God their Shepherd. Notice the repetition of the word "my" and read Ezek. 34 : 31 in this connection, also Jer. 31 : 3.

Why is it that people are so slow to believe that the heavenly Father is as He is described in this chapter? What effect would it have on the hearts of people if they really grasped the truth about God's yearning, seeking love? If it is true that we belong to God as His own, what effect should it have on our daily attitude of mind? Read Psalm 23 for a picture of one who realized this truth. If any of His sheep have lost their way and turned their back on their Shepherd, where may we expect to find Him? What is the only course open to a Shepherd who cares for the sheep as He does?

II. *God still seeking through Jesus Christ.*

Read John 10 : 1–18. Notice again the reiteration of the words "his own," "mine own" in verses 3 and 14 and the challenge to the hireling "whose own the sheep are *not*." In verses 8 and 14 why is it that the sheep know the voice of the Shepherd rather than the voice of a robber? Read verse 9 in the light of the solemn warning given by our Lord in Luke 13 : 24. How may we be sure that we have entered the door?

What experiences with God will the sheep have, according to this chapter, if they recognize and accept the ownership of their Shepherd Jesus Christ? Notice the outreach of the Shepherd's love in verse 16 and the intensity of His yearning in the words, "I *must* bring."

How does the Shepherd earn the right to claim the sheep as His own in verse 11?

True love must always meet the test of suffering vicariously on behalf of the loved one, or it is unworthy of the name. The picture of the heart of God as the Good Shepherd has forever defined love in its reality.

III. *The love of the Good Shepherd an individual personal love.*

Read Matt. 18 : 10–14 and Luke 15 : 1–10.

Note: (1) The love of the Shepherd seeks the one that is lost before it wants to be found. (2) The love of the Shepherd knows no limit "until he find it." (3) What must the value of one individual be to be worth the utmost of sacrifice! (4) The sheep belonged to the Shepherd even while it was lost from the fold. "I have found my sheep which *was* lost." It is the appeal of the suffering, anxious love of God that those who have lost their way in this world need to hear, in order that they may come to themselves and be found of Him. "We love because he first loved us" (I John 4 : 19).

What called forth the three parables in the fifteenth chapter of Luke? See verses 1 and 2. How does this reveal the crowning gift of true love?

IV. *The expectation of the Good Shepherd that His friends will share His spirit.*

Read Matt. 9 : 36–10 : 1, and John 4 : 35.

Note: (1) Jesus Christ begins to teach His disciples to look at the multitudes with His eyes; to see beneath the surface into their troubled, unsatisfied hearts; to see the fields ripe for the harvest. (2) The command to pray that laborers be sent into the harvest is significant in that the prayer develops, in the hearts of those who utter it, the same spirit of compassion and yearning that in the end will send them forth into the harvest. The prayer is not a petition to overcome any reluctance of God to thrust out laborers but the birth of a dominant desire and spirit that will bring the intercessors into oneness of spirit with God, and issue in one united purpose to redeem the world.

V. *Jesus Christ applies the test of true love to His disciple.*

Read John 21 : 15–17. In this we see the purpose of our Lord that we, too, should follow in His steps and shepherd the sheep in His name. The motive to which He appeals is not the need of the sheep, although He had taught His disciples to discern that; but He tests the reality of our personal love for Him by its spirit of vicarious sacrifice for those whom He loves. From that time on whenever we yearn to see a life redeemed unto God it is the spirit of our Lord yearning in and through us. So in truth it was said of the disciples: "They went forth, and preached everywhere, the Lord working with them" (Mark 16 : 20).

> "O tender Shepherd climbing rugged mountains
> And crossing waters deep—
> How long wouldst Thou be willing to go homeless
> To find a straying sheep?
> I count no time, the Shepherd gently answered,
> As thou dost count and bind
> The weeks in months, the months in years,—
> My counting is just—until I find.
> And that would be the limit of My journey—
> I'd cross the waters deep,
> And climb the hillsides with unfailing patience
> Until I find My sheep."

CHAPTER IV

PREPARATION FOR SERVICE

We have faced our obligations as Christians to help in interpreting the Christian life to others, and we have seen how inevitable and natural it is that we should do this when we remember the simple axioms of our faith; now we are faced by the necessity for personal preparation. We do not want to bungle when we might be skilful. Failing a perfect instrument God might use with power even a blunt and rusty blade, but He can do more with one that is perfectly adapted for use. Our ability to help depends on our knowledge of human life, as well as on our knowledge of God and on our wisdom in bringing one in relation to the other so that the best wisdom at our disposal is none too good for what we are undertaking.

A full preparation for fellowship with Christ in winning His kingdom cannot be attained in a given time. It is a life process and grows with experience in actual service. Books and training-classes are valuable only in so far as they suggest fields for conquest and help us to begin the service with a rational and intelligent point of view.

At the outset let us rid ourselves of the notion that one can acquire a mechanical process or set of rules by which people can be brought into the kingdom of God. We are not asked to tell others what they ought to do, but to live a life of undisguised loyalty to our Lord. Only the outflow and overflow of a Christ-controlled life will create in another life a thirst for Christ. That woman in India illustrated this fact when she said to a Christian missionary: "If your Jesus is like you I want to know Him." There is much professional, officious intrusion into the sanctity of another life under the garb of a sincere interest in another's spiritual welfare. It smacks of professionalism and cant and is usually interpreted justly as an impertinence. Because of this the sacred service of relating a life to Jesus Christ has often been brought into disrepute among sensitive and sincere Christians. "How can a person be courteous and considerate and venture to intrude upon another life even though she comes in the name of Christ?" was a question asked by an earnest student who longed to obey Christ's command. The answer is a simple one. Do not intrude but wait for that moment when there will be some spontaneous self-revelation to which you must respond. Let it be your chief concern to yield daily implicit obedience to the loving guidance of Christ, keep yourself in the atmosphere of purity, peace, and childlike trust and then live your daily life steadily and openly. Be constantly alert and watchful, concerned that others may know Christ and quickly ready to use any opportunity that may come to interpret Him to another heart by deed or word. We may not say, "I have this afternoon free and I will use it to make Christ known to individuals." The times and seasons are not in our hands. It is the Spirit of God alone who can so relate two people that His life may be imparted as if through a live wire.

There is no release from this service. Every day and every hour in the day we must be ready and responsive. There are times when one needs to take the initiative. This is pre-eminently true in the case of teachers with pupils or in those closer personal relationships with our friends. It is easier to maintain the accepted even level of friendship than constantly to deepen that level. It is the office of a friend to hold one to one's best. The greatest stimulus toward the best will be found in a mutual sharing of the sources of our strength, the purposes of our heart, and our growing friendship with Christ. Some of our days are rich with opportunities for quiet walks and talks with friends. Who can measure the power of friendships based on fellowship with Jesus Christ?

As we face some of the ways in which we need to prepare ourselves for successful service the following points seem essential:

We must have a steadfast relation with Christ as a personal Saviour and Master. Mere opinions or theories or inherited beliefs concerning Christianity will not suffice. We cannot give another what we ourselves do not possess. Paul suggests this truth in his letter to the Romans in the words: "For I will not dare to speak of any things save those which Christ wrought through me . . . by word and deed" (Romans 15 : 18). An honest desire to serve must lead one to search one's heart to see whether one has a real and living experience with God.

The honest confession to God of all known sin is necessary. There must be also an increasing sensitiveness to the presence of sin, a relentless fight against it, and a conviction of ultimate victory through Jesus Christ. It is not our perfection of character that wins another to Christ but the faithful struggle toward perfection. It is this that makes it possible for imperfect man rather than the morally perfect angels of God to help in redeeming the world. David voices this in his marvellous prayer: "Create in me a clean heart, O God; and renew a right spirit within me. Cast me not away from thy presence; and take not thy Holy Spirit from me. Restore unto me the joy of thy salvation, and uphold me with a willing Spirit. *Then* will I teach transgressors thy ways and sinners shall be converted unto thee" (Psalm 51 : 10–13).

We need also to have a clearly defined conception of the normal Christian experience. The essential elements may be stated as follows:

(*a*) A vision of the holiness of God and the moral requirements of His character.

(*b*) A conviction of personal need—that "I have sinned and fall short of the glory of God" (Romans 3 : 23).

(*c*) An acceptance of forgiveness and cleansing through the sacrifice of Jesus Christ—"the Son of God who loved me and gave himself for me" (Gal. 2 : 20).

(*d*) A daily dependence on divine power for spiritual growth.

(*e*) A desire for service which makes one long to co-operate with God in carrying out His purposes for the world.

On these foundation-stones God builds individual experiences each differing from the other. No two will be precisely alike, and we cannot expect that people will come to Christ through the same experiences or in the same way. Any one of the essential elements may be the starting-point of the Christian life. For example, one may see a community need or a person in sore straits and long to help, only to discover that one needs to be linked up with God before attempting to help the souls of people. It will be like the man in the parable who came saying: "Friend, lend me three loaves of bread, for a friend of mine is come to me in his journey *and I have nothing to set before him.*" In like manner the story of the life and death of

Jesus Christ may bring a conviction of personal need, or it may be the challenge of some moral requirement. A friend once said that her careless, purposeless life was changed from the time when she heard in church one day the challenge of the Psalm: "Who shall ascend into the hill of the Lord and who shall stand in his holy place? He that hath clean hands and a pure heart" (Psalm 24 : 3, 4). The words haunted her for days until she gave herself to God to receive a new life and a clean heart. Although in each case the sequence of experience is different, the essential elements are the same.

It is an essential part of our preparation also that we should have an increasing knowledge of the Bible. We must know the teachings of Jesus, the record of God's dealings with human nature through all the ages, and the experiences of the apostles in interpreting Christ to the world. This does not mean that we need the equivalent of a theological course, although that is valuable, but it does mean that we shall begin with what we know and then by faithful study increase our knowledge of God by natural growth. A crude, ignorant woman who lived on the east side of New York and knew only one verse in the Bible, which she learned at a mission, was able to bring five of her women friends into a Christian life with that verse as a foundation for their faith. It was the word of God to them and they acted on it. Thus God uses the little we have if it is all we have, but it is only the beginning of what He may do through us as we add knowledge and experience day by day. It is not necessary for others to know our own thoughts; but God's thoughts, paraphrased by our experience, have the power to transform a life into likeness to Jesus Christ. Therefore we need to be sure that we are measuring our life and character by the plumb-line of Jesus' life.

One of the severest chapters in the Bible is that section in the prophecy of Jeremiah which says concerning the teachers of that day: "They speak a vision of their own heart, and not out of the mouth of Jehovah. . . . I spake not unto them yet they prophesied. But if they had stood in my councils then had they caused my people to hear my words, and had turned them from their evil way" (Jer. 23 : 16). And the solemn warning comes: "The prophet that hath a dream let him tell a dream; and he that hath my word, let him speak my word faithfully. What is straw to the wheat? saith Jehovah."

It is also important that we train our powers of observation to understand the laws of human nature. This comes with experience, but can be increased in us by trying sympathetically to understand the point of view of other people. We must not be distracted by outward appearance, but learn to read the hidden meanings behind the outward expressions. In the free social relationships of modern life it is not difficult to get at the inner point of view, for it is unconsciously revealed in so many little ways. The kind of pleasures that people turn to for rest; the friends they like to be with, the books they enjoy, the clothes they wear are all indications of character. The study of oneself and one's natural reactions to certain influences is a fruitful means of studying human nature. The counsel of Jesus, "Whatsoever ye would that men should do unto you, even so do ye also unto them" (Matt. 7 : 12), is a sure guide. It is only as we diagnose ourselves that we can respond to the craving of others for honest sympathy and sympathetic honesty.

We must also have a right attitude toward the experiences of life. In other words, we must learn to see God in relation to the circumstances of our lives. Unless we have learned to see our lives as fulfilling a divine plan and purpose, we shall be likely to miss the meaning of much that comes to us and thus be unable to help others. If other people instead of God are the norm by which we judge relative values we shall have no poise and peace in life. Our attitude toward our limitations, toward our possessions, toward suffering, toward restrictions of circumstances, and toward our opportunities must be based on the certainty that our Father holds all in His control for our highest good or we cannot help others who are in the clutch of selfish desires to find peace by accepting God's plan for their lives. Nothing so marks the difference between a child of God and a child of the world as the varying attitudes toward the experiences of life. There is a powerful witness in a life which actually lives out the words:

> "What Thou shalt to-day provide
> Let me as a child receive,—
> What to-morrow shall betide
> Calmly to Thy wisdom leave.
> 'Tis enough that Thou wilt care;
> Why should I the burden bear?"

A quiet courage coupled with freedom from ulterior motives is also imperative. The ruling desire must be for the extension of Christ's kingdom and not for personal success. It is not success but faithfulness that one must covet, and the courage of brave persistence. We must sink ourselves in the message:

> "Not I but Christ, be honored, loved, exalted;
> Not I but Christ, be seen, be known, be heard;
> Not I but Christ, in every look and action;
> Not I but Christ, in every thought and word."

Our efficiency will depend largely on our flexibility and teachableness. There should be no dogmatism, no insistence on a personal view-point. It is the work of God's Spirit to lead into the truth and we must be patient when that work seems slowly done. It is an exquisite art, well worth coveting, to know when to press the claims of Christ and at the same time to be utterly free from any domination of another's will or personality by one's own intensity of will-power. We need to guard against forcing a hothouse growth in a plant that must stand the rigors of an outdoor life.

Every one who would do important service must be prepared to live a sacrificial life. Everything that is worth while costs something. To the one whose eyes are on the goal the price is incidental. Every doctor makes himself aseptic if he expects to be trusted with the issues of human life. There are certain things he may not do just because he has the important service to perform. In like manner we must be willing to make ourselves spiritually aseptic if we are to be trusted with important service. This does not mean that there is any virtue in refraining from legitimate things just for the sake of refraining. It is only when we practise self-denial for a purpose that it is worth while. Our ability to help another depends on our power of spiritual discernment. Such discernment depends largely on our sensitiveness of spirit toward God, which may be cultivated or dulled by our habits of life. In fact, much of our shrinking from the task of helping others to know God comes from the consciousness that we are not ready, that our garments are not "unspotted from the world," and that our communion has been interrupted by what we have been doing. Books that coarsen our ideals or blur our moral standards unfit us to touch people's hearts. Practices that lower the moral tone and leave a disquieting conscience take away the fresh spiritual vigor. Without this readiness to pay the price we shall never be able to influence people deeply for the kingdom of God. In fact we shall have to be willing to obey implicitly the directions of Paul when he said: "Whatsoever things are true, whatsoever things are honorable, whatsoever things are just, whatsoever things are pure, whatsoever things are lovely, whatsoever things are of good report, if there be any praise, if there be any virtue, think on these things."

Finally, it is especially important, in the delicate task of interpreting Christ to another, that we should realize that an inner sense of weakness is the normal state of a Christian. We need never expect that we shall feel adequate for our task. This sense of weakness keeps one dependent on God's power; it keeps one humble, it develops tact through increasing sensitiveness to atmosphere; it is a constant reminder that any success or power is of God alone. Fortunate will it be for us if in all our preparation for service we learn this lesson well and have a simple, childlike faith in the truth of what Paul learned, "My power is made perfect in weakness," and are able to respond in calm trust: "Wherefore I take pleasure in weaknesses . . . for when I am weak, then am I strong" (II Cor. 12 : 9–10).

BIBLE STUDY IV

Right Attitudes in Service

I. *A right attitude toward life's experiences and limitations as a training-school for character.*

(1) *Toward affliction and trouble.*—Read I Cor. 1 : 4. What preparation for service does Paul suggest as a compensation for suffering? How do the words in Heb. 2 : 10–11 read new meaning in the word *"brethren"?* How is this reinforced by Heb. 4 : 15, 16. What is the full content of the word *"therefore"* in verse 16? What confidence does it give us? Read II Cor. 4 : 7–10. How do these experiences keep us from spiritual pride and reveal to others the power of God? See II Cor. 4 : 17, 18 for another reason why trouble is of value to us as servants of God.

(2) *Toward our limitations.*—Read II Cor. 6 : 10. Why is it necessary to acquire a new sense of values in order to serve others in Christ's name? See II Cor. 8 : 9. There is an advantage in the limitations of circumstances when they are sincerely accepted, because we can then establish simple human relations free from false barriers. We also have freedom then to make the spiritual appeal dominant with no ulterior motives.

(3) *Toward our critics and enemies, as an opportunity to release the Father's spirit.*—Read Matt. 5 : 44, 45. Love is the object-lesson which demon-

strates the Father's spirit to the world. See also John 17 : 21. Why is love a proof that Jesus Christ has come into the world?

(4) *Toward our weaknesses and inadequacy.*—Read I Cor. 2 : 3-5 and II Cor. 12 : 9-10. Weakness is the normal state of a Christian because it keeps us humbly dependent on God. Read James 1 : 5 as a challenge to the exercise of faith. See also II Cor. 3 : 4-6 and II Cor. 2 : 14. Is not weakness worth while if it makes possible the exhilaration of spiritual triumph?

II. *A right attitude of sincerity about ourselves.*

Read Phil. 3 : 12. Do we lose or gain influence by an honest confession of our imperfection? Why will people be helped more by one who is making progress in the carrying out of a purpose than by one who has attained the goal? See I John 1 : 3. What should be the purpose of our relationships with people? Is it imparting light or entering into a comradeship?

III. *The right attitude toward sin.*

See Psalm 51 : 10-13. "Create in me a clean heart . . . then will I teach transgressors thy ways," etc. What is the effect of sin in the heart? See Psalm 66 : 18-19. Sin is the word used to describe the moral sense of failing to measure up to God's standard; therefore the conviction of the conscience in respect to sin is only the work of God's Spirit. The sense of sin deepens as the knowledge of the character of God increases. Sin prevents our fellowship with God and separates us from the intimate communion with Him.

IV. *The right attitude toward the teaching of Christ as a correction for one's own opinions.*

Read I Cor. 2 : 1-5 and Heb. 4 : 12-13. We need to face the moral challenge of the teachings of Christ and not merely be familiar with them. What was the great fault of the people who heard Jesus speak in John 7 : 37-43? What is the common danger in religious discussion? Think over the value of II Tim. 3 : 14-17 as a training for service. In verse 16 the word "instruction" is rendered in the Greek "discipline in righteousness." To what degree are our failures in character due to the neglect of this teaching?

CHAPTER V

SOME LAWS THAT CONDITION MENTAL REACTIONS

Most of us, at some time or other, have agreed with the old Quaker who said to "his better half": "All the world is queer, Rachel, except thee and me, and sometimes I think thee also is a little queer." Human nature has seemed erratic and askew and "there is no accounting for it," we say. This is largely due to our ignorance of the natural laws by which the mind works. Modern psychology has put into our hands the means of getting at the truth about human nature. It helps us to see how precisely the mind reacts to a given stimulus if we know its basic laws. As we look at Jesus Christ, who "knew what was in man," we are awed by the exquisite tact with which He knew how to appeal to people in the way that was natural and human and irresistible. His methods were rational and He used instinctively those principles which we, twenty centuries later, stumble upon with the help of psychologists and hail as a new discovery. Slowly but surely we are finding new guides for our faith, and we are more ready to yield to the reasonableness of the teaching of Christ. No student of human nature can shirk the study of these natural laws and hope to understand people.

There is a right way and a wrong way to do everything. For example, there is a right way to pick up a kitten and there is a wrong way; and the disposition of the kitten and her affection toward you is quite dependent upon the way you handle her. So with human beings; there is a right and wrong way to touch the mind and personality of every one. In our Christian work we are responsible for the antagonisms we call forth as well as for the assents. We can reduce to a minimum the adverse reactions if we understand the natural laws by which a mind works.

In so brief a space as this there can be stated only a few of these elemental principles in simple terms as an aid in our efforts to help others to know God. A fuller discussion can be found in any of the text-books of psychology.

(1) *The mind is controlled more completely by positives than negatives. It tends to yield to the suggestion of "do" rather than "don't."* This law has not always been observed by religious teachers, who have pictured the Christian life as a series of negatives, as a life so cabined and confined and repressed that it had no outlet for its powers. The gospel of Christ has often been preached as if it were endless advice about what one must "give up" in order to find peace. The gloom of negative sin instead of the light of positive goodness has been talked, and then one has wondered why people did not naturally respond to it. The people were only acting naturally as God made them, and were just waiting like plants to turn away from the dark whenever the positive light of the sun drew them. We have only to look back into the history of our own religious experience to find illustrations of the results of this negative system.

Sooner or later the normal mind is likely to react from this negative view and will in the end follow whatever positive teaching is presented to it. One is always in a state of unstable equilibrium when the attention is held merely by "Thou shalt nots." Sometimes we wonder why Christians of mature years suddenly leave their church and take up some new cult and vagary in religious teaching. The reason is a simple one. That cult, because of its emphasis on one idea, may have been the first positive teaching that ever made a dent on the mind, and the years of restraint and negative teaching had so pent up the soul that it had to make a dash for what it thought to be liberty, without stopping to see whether the new faith was logical and reasonable. Thus the mind is made for action rather than for restraint. One must do to know. "He that willeth to *do* my will shall know the teaching," says Jesus, not "He that keeps from doing what is not my will." The best and only effective way to keep from doing what is wrong is to do something else that is right; this is the only way in which to focus the attention of mind; it must be held by something positive. We shall see how this principle works out in forms of religious experience later on. We must centre the attention upon the great constructive work that calls forth all our powers so that they are not available for the positive suggestions of evil.

(2) *One must always take into account the differences in temperament.* We are not all alike; each has his own mental bias. Fundamentally we are alike, but our temperamental qualities are combined in different proportions. Thus, while we all possess intellectual, volitional, and emotional qualities, we differ in the way in which these qualities are blended in us. We may be strong in one quality and weak in others. Thus the needs and temptations of people will vary according to their temperamental emphasis. No one counsel will meet the need of all. If a person is stronger intellectually than he is volitionally he will be tempted to be interested in religious teachings without facing their moral challenge for a new life; to preach without practising, to be dogmatic without compassion. Such people need to face the message of Jesus when He said: "Not every one that saith unto me, Lord, Lord, shall enter into the kingdom of heaven, but he that doeth the will of my Father who is in heaven" (Matt. 7 : 21), or "Blessed are the merciful: for they shall obtain mercy" (Matt. 5 : 7). Similarly, the person in whom the volitional element is dominant will be tempted to be stubborn and wilful and resist the voice of God. Such individuals need to face the test of Jesus' words: "He that doth not take his cross and follow after me, is not worthy of me" (Matt. 10 : 38). People who are strongly developed emotionally are likely to be guilty of sentimentality and selfishness and need the tonic of those ringing words: "He that hath my commandments and keepeth them, he it is that loveth me" (John 14 : 21).

In a similar manner the natural expression of the Christian life will differ according to temperament and one is not likely to have the same religious experience as another.

The citadel of opposition to God's control of the life will vary according to the dominant qualities of temperament. Suppose one were trying to win a strongly volitional temperament to the control of God's Spirit. The centre of resistance will naturally lie in the will, for that is the strong point. The line of least resistance will be found in the affections or in an appeal to the reason, and such people find it easy to yield their wills when their hearts are touched by the love of Christ. In the same way the emotional temperament is led by an appeal to yield the will to God and thus to find that steadying power for a new life where the emotions will be controllable. This will also be true for the intellectual temperament who will be tempted to inconclusive thinking unless the will is yielded to God for a new dynamic. The advantage of a personal conversation over a public sermon lies in the fact that one can adapt the appeal to the temperament of the individual and thus get a fuller response.

(3) *In all religious work we must take full account of the laws of habit in dealing with problems of moral and religious life.* A simple acknowledgment of faith does not reverse all one's life habits at once. That is a process which requires many years, not a moment of time. By one act of the will one may decide to yield oneself wholly to the control of Jesus Christ, but the working out of that control is a matter of years, because that decision will have to encounter life habits and processes that will cut across and contradict all the decisions of the best self.

One must take this into account in helping people religiously. We must be prepared for disappointments, or rather we must not set up an expectation that will have to be disappointed. Take for granted that the decision is perfectly true, sincere, and clear, and that it will work itself out slowly in spite of waverings until finally it becomes steady and dominant in the heart. The religious life of many of us is like the magnetic needle of the compass that quivers toward the north and in spite of vibrations is held true to the pole. It is not the flickering of the will at a given moment that shows the real truth but the habitual return to purpose.

It would be well for us to reread often that classic discussion of "Habit" in Professor James's *Principles of Psychology* and learn how to "make our nervous system our ally instead of our enemy." New habits have to be built up which will displace old ones. New tracks have to be made between nerve-centres that will help us in the end to "do good naturally" without inner struggles of will. The value of surrounding ourselves with "means of grace" and cutting off old associations that stifle the new life becomes increasingly apparent. We must commit ourselves utterly to the new cause of living a holy life without turning back. We must refuse to feed the springs of wrong desires, and we must act on every holy purpose we form and on every inner voice of conscience. No matter how many purposes we may have and no matter how good our sentiments may be, if we do not take advantage of every concrete opportunity to act, our characters may remain entirely unaffected for the better.

It is necessary, too, that we learn to discipline our spirits in doing each day some service that we are not obliged to do but which we want to do merely for the sake of moral training. We need to build up a moral margin of strength for the unusual strain that we may have to stand some day.

Adolescent days are the time when life habits become fixed and when the character of one's whole life is determined. By voluntary acts of the will we reaffirm the habits of childhood or make new ones. Fortunate is that one who yields the will so completely to the irresistible Christ that all habits of life spring from a supreme Christian purpose.

In spite of the grim truth that each day we are forging chains of habit that will either make us permanently strong or permanently weak, wrong habits can be remade by the power of God. New habits can be formed if a new motive is found in the heart, and the truth of Saint Paul's words will be realized anew: "If any man is in Christ, there is a new creation: the old things are passed away; behold they are become new" (II Cor. 5 : 17).

(4) *It must be remembered also that we are so made that mental and physical states are interrelated.* Weakness of character often has its secret in physical limitations. Physical conditions largely determine our mental bias and affect the buoyancy of our faith. An enervated body depresses the mind and warps the judgment. It weakens our power of concentration and thus breaks down our moral resistance, so that we fall an easy prey to swift temptations. In the same way some unwholesome emotion or mental obsession reacts on the body and undermines its health. There are many people who will never have strong bodies until they have a mental and spiritual life infilled with God's peace and poise, possible only through a vital relationship with Jesus Christ. It is also true that many will never be able to overcome certain temptations or live a life of faith until they correct the physical weaknesses that result from hectic habits of living and build up enough nervous energy to reinforce the spirit in times of crisis. We have no

right to ignore this interrelationship of mind and body or to neglect the conditions that supply that essential moral margin. In this way only shall we be able to meet the strain of daily living and unusual exigencies. Therefore it often happens that the most help we can bring to any one at the beginning is definite counsel about safeguarding the nervous energy one has and increasing it. This will be discussed more fully in another chapter.

(5) *In dealing with the religious life of any one we can count upon the help of the subconscious life as well as the response of the conscious attention.* By far the larger part of our mental life is beyond and beneath the small area of our conscious attention. This subconscious mind is the storehouse for all our mental impressions, desires, prejudices, and forgotten experiences. Influences that have been unnoticed and all things that are latent are found there. We may not be at all conscious of paying attention to these impressions, but they sink down into our subconsciousness, and some day, by the natural law of the association of ideas, they may compel our attention and rule our choices. The conscious attention of a person may be focussed intently on certain interests that conflict with the claims of the spiritual life. Indifference toward God and opposition to His will may be the apparent state of the heart; when, lo! some chance word or experience may call up a new chain of ideas and holy memories that may sweep over the mind like a flood and compel the heart to face its God.

This reinforcement of the subconscious life ought to increase our faith and courage because of the way in which it works. It gives new worth to what a religious atmosphere can do for a child or any one, in that it makes an unconscious impression on the mind which may be a powerful factor in the decision of the will later on. It makes every Bible class and religious service significant in that it increases the assets which can be drawn upon in temptation or need. We are sometimes surprised at the seeming effect on character of a few words which catch the attention of some one we would help. The probability is that those few words were only powerful in that they released a whole train of thoughts and memories that surged in upon the attention from forgotten depths and all together led that individual to make a supreme decision for God. This makes even incidental conversation significant, for one never knows what it will call forth.

This storehouse of memories and impulses is peculiarly accessible to the Spirit of God, who works within us "to will and to do His good pleasure," "bringing to our remembrance" whatsoever God is saying to us. Therefore in all our work for others we can count upon our words of appeal being reinforced by memories and associations which the Spirit of God brings to the attention of the conscious self.

(6) *In the religious life the fundamental motive that moves the will is love.* This love may be directed toward God, or toward self, or toward others. Sometimes the heart is moved by love toward God, through its gratitude for the blessings of life, for guidance through difficulties and protection from unseen dangers. Or it may be through the conscious love of beauty that the heart is drawn toward the God of nature. Perhaps, too, the pressure of the social needs of humanity may create a sympathy and love for the person of our Lord who gave Himself to seek and save those who had wandered away.

In a similar way the love of self may be a motive to turn the will toward God through a fear lest, having gained the whole world, one may lose his soul. Ambition and a desire to make the most of life may also lead one to seek God, and a self-respecting spirit may drive some people to be Christians merely from a sense of honor.

The love of others is a compelling motive for most people. The sense of responsibility for another life, the love of a mother or friend has pulled many men and women away from unworthy lives and turned them to God for help. People who never dreamed of seeking God for themselves are eager for help and light when they are face to face with some one who needs their help. It is fortunate that we are unable to meet the need of even one life with our own resources, for it is the sense of utter helplessness in the face of the life problems of others near to us that brings us to God with the cry of the man described by our Lord in the parable: "A friend of mine is come to me from a journey, and I have nothing to set before him" (Luke 11 : 6).

BIBLE STUDY V

SOME INDIVIDUALS WHO CAME TO KNOW CHRIST

I. *An outcast.*

Read John 4 : 1–29. The woman of Samaria. Verses 6, 7. Note our Lord's alertness in seeing the need of another; although wearied from the journey yet ready to meet any human need. What was His natural method of approach? Note that in asking this favor of the Samarian outcast, Jesus invested her with the dignity of a hostess to whom one would be under obligation. What do the expectations of others call forth in us? See verses 9–18. Point out the ways in which Jesus showed His gentleness and exquisite tact in creating first a curiosity and desire for living water before reminding her of her sin. Then in verses 19–26 mark His unwillingness to be diverted from the main point and getting at the heart of the secret life which the Father "who seeth in secret" desires as His temple made clean and fit for His indwelling. How does the last clause of verse 23 bring a sense of dignity and worth to the woman's life?

II. *A distinguished traveller.*

Read Acts 8 : 26–30. Here the opportunity to preach the message of Jesus Christ comes to a man who is alert and listening to the inner guiding spirit. If God looks upon the heart and sees in it a desire to know the truth, is it not a simple matter for Him to bring help through any disciple who is listening for His inner impulse. The outcome of this conversation with the eunuch made Philip know that he had been guided. If we are really ready to be used at any moment we will find many a casual journey directed by God, even though we may be unconscious of it. How can we be sure every day that our steps are directed by God? Have we the right to expect that every path of duty and right is part of God's plan for us? If this is so, why do we not find more opportunities to reveal Christ along the way?

In verses 30 and 31 note the tact of Philip's first question. It is natural and not intrusive and inspires a desire for help. Philip did not impose his help upon the eunuch, but gives him a chance to speak out his point of view. This at once produces the natural desire for an exchange of thought. In verse 35 Philip begins at the point where he was reading; the point of contact from which a natural development of conversation is possible. Why is it that an argument usually fails to give people much help? Why is it always wise to begin with people at the point of their present interest? Write out an outline of what you think Philip might have said from his text in verses 32 and 33. How would you preach Jesus Christ to a seeker after truth from this text? What must have been the last point in Philip's conversation? See verse 36.

III. *The man who toiled for his daily bread.*

Read Luke 5 : 1–11. In verse 3 what might have been in the mind of Jesus when He went into Simon's boat instead of the other? What would the fact that Jesus was in his boat call out in Simon? Notice the skill of Jesus in winning Simon, in recognizing Simon's leadership and asking a service within his power; thus enlisting his interest and loyalty to the one who was a guest in his boat. Simon was close to Jesus in the boat, co-operating in helping the people get the message, and was won in spite of himself. What was the crowning evidence to Simon that here was one who could be trusted? Why was it necessary for Jesus to manifest his power in the sphere where Simon had most power? What is it that produces a spirit of humility in any one?

In these three cases the disciple was won through the willing obedience to the truth spoken. This co-operation of the will which is essential was secured at the outset through, first, a strong desire stimulated by curiosity; second, by a childlike, teachable spirit called forth by the tact of Philip; third, through loyalty to the obligations of hospitality. In each case the *best* was called forth and used to win discipleship. Can you think of people who are inaccessible to the appeal of Christ because some worker has called out opposition and prejudice at the start? Notice that to each of these three people the approach was made in confidence that they were at *heart* comrades.

CHAPTER VI

THE DEVELOPMENT OF A NORMAL CHRISTIAN EXPERIENCE

It is not an easy task to discuss this subject. Christian experience is so intimate and sacred that it shrinks from ordinary scrutiny and it is not possible to measure and weigh the things of the Spirit with usual standards. Moreover, the touch of God in the life is so delicate and often so hidden from consciousness that it is not possible to trace it accurately. When we remember, too, that the temperamental differences in individuals give rise to an infinite variety of Christian experiences in which certain processes are either lengthened or shortened, and that their experiences often lie in the unfathomed depths of the subconscious mind, we realize that no discussion of so varied a problem can be adequate.

However, the elements of the Christian life are real and are eternal verities. No analysis of them can change their nature. In fact, their reality is proven all the more if we can discover the orderly methods by which God works in our hearts to develop in us a Christian experience.

The background and general development of a person's religious life must always be taken into account before one is able to give help at any time of crisis. The law of cause and effect works so precisely that we need to know this background before we can see where there has been a deviation from a normal Christian experience and how a life can be restored to a normal relationship with God.

Every child that is born into the world has a capacity to know God and a spiritual instinct for God. It is, as John says, "that true Light that lighteth every man that cometh into the world" (John 1 : 9). A little child does not resist the teaching about the heavenly Father who is revealed to us by Jesus Christ. Children are so near the spiritual world that they accept it naturally. The life of the child, unresisting toward these divine impulses and drawings, is the ideal which our Lord had in mind when He said: "Whosoever shall not receive the kingdom of God as a little child, he shall in no wise enter therein" (Mark 10 : 15). If the parents have begun from the first to train the child in self-control and obedience, helping it to understand that the principles of right and wrong are God's teaching to which both old and young owe reverence and obedience, a broad foundation for a normal Christian life will have been laid. Sooner or later the day will come when the developing self-consciousness of the child will break out in a deliberate refusal to obey the will of the parent, who is the unifying authority of the family social group. This is the first real crisis in the spiritual life of the child.

We cannot appreciate the significance of this crisis without thinking a moment of the relation between the individual and society. At certain times in our experience each has seemed to exclude the other. As individuals we have been afraid of being directed by the will of the social group lest we lose our individuality and give up that personal freedom which is our inherent right. Gradually, however, it dawns upon us that our sense of individuality grows clearly defined only as we measure swords with the wills and opinions of others. We then find the strength of our own wills and see ourselves in true perspective. There would be nothing to call out this self-assertion if we lived alone on a desert island; we find ourselves only in our relationships with the social group. This is why the family is the ideal setting for the child. Opposition of wills, therefore, is natural and a sign of growing individuality.

At this point we come to a parting of the ways and our future depends on the path we take. The first time we meet this crisis is at that period of childhood when we consciously and deliberately question the will of the parent. Our present religious experience is largely colored by the way in which our parents met this crisis. Perhaps the will of the child won and the authority of the family group was weakened; perhaps the will of the parent overcame and suppressed the will of the child and compelled blind obedience. Either of these methods results in moral weakness. Fortunate, indeed, is that child whose family group has been so ideal that this opposition of wills is turned into a co-operation of wills whereby the highest good is possible both for the child and the family social group.

In this way a child may enter into its first conscious experience with God, through a co-operation of will.

This co-operation is best secured by developing in the child a loyal reverence for the will of God and His moral teaching, to which all His children owe obedience. In other words, if at the time of wilful refusal to obey the child realizes that the will with which he is asked to co-operate is not only the will or whim of the parent but is a concrete interpretation of God's teaching, a basis for a lasting peace and for the highest individual development is secured. As this co-operation must be secured if the child is to find its highest self-realization, the issue of obedience or disobedience is all-important. If at the time of the refusal to obey the wise will of the parent the parent secures obedience, then the normal growth of the child's spiritual life is assured; if through weakness or mistaken love the parent lets the "clash of wills" abide, then a sense of sin develops. The child is conscious of the ever-widening break in its oneness and fellowship with its parent and with God, and repeated instances of disobedience only widen the gulf and harden the heart of the child to spiritual appeal.

Many children grow up to be adults without ever having co-operated willingly in obedience in all their experience. Their spiritual weakness is pitiful; their wills have become stubborn; they are in a continual state of rebellion and discontent with God and His purposes, they are conscious of hopeless discouragement, something seems "always wrong" with them. All this inheritance from an unconquered youth they have to bear in addition to the serious questions of adult life which require an open mind and a reverent, obedient will. Much so-called intellectual difficulty in matters of Christian faith is rooted in an undisciplined spirit that has rebelled so steadily in disobedience to parents that it inevitably questions even God's methods and purposes. Christian mothers little realize how they are handicapping the future of their children when they do not help their children to meet their first spiritual crisis and win a full victory of willing obedience at a time when it is easier than it ever will be later.

Various motives may help a child to face its need for an obedient co-operative will. It may be a fear of consequences that deters for the time being, until some higher considerations win the child's loyalty; it may be a love that cannot bear to have the intimacy of relationship withdrawn and therefore forces the will to yield. Or the compelling motive may be the prick of an inner conscience that knows that God is right and that His standard of conduct ought to prevail. Fortunate is the child that has been trained to have such a conscience, for out of this experience comes the sense of personal need and the spirit of penitence and teachableness that makes the highest self-development possible. In fact, the recognition of personal shortcomings is part of the spiritual process of regeneration; the new attitude of mind that issues in a will to obey the entreaties of the Spirit of God and begin a new life.

The value of keeping before children the moral standards of God cannot be overestimated as a help in training a sensitive conscience and securing a co-operative will. The Old Testament stories of men and women who had vivid, clear-cut experiences with the elemental laws of God and who were as human as we are, are of special value for the religious teaching of children. The perfection of the life of Jesus Christ is all the more radiant in comparison. A group of dirty children were once playing in an East Side street, when out of a house came a little girl dressed in spotless white, going with her mother on a visit. One of the children dropped the hands of the others and stood looking wistfully at the little girl in white, and as she gazed at her quite unconsciously her hand reached back and pulled the corner of her apron over a big soiled place in front. There were no words spoken, but a woman passing by saw a spiritual process going on—a general need for cleanliness had become a personal longing in that little spirit, through the sight of a perfect standard.

The sense of personal longing for a life more pleasing to God brings a teachable spirit that results in a dedication of oneself to a renewed obedience to the teaching of God. This results in a closer fellowship with Him, in which prayer becomes a communion, in which there is no sense of barriers. God is accessible and increasingly near and the life becomes buoyant and free, growing in love and a desire to serve Him. This ought to be the normal life of a Christian child up to the time of adult life, expressing itself simply in obedience, reverence, love, and service.

As one grows into adult life the full responsibility of making one's own decisions comes as a new experience. The former authority of parents in all matters of decision becomes inadequate in the face of responsibilities to other social groups in business, college, society, *et cetera*, and the Christian youth must find a new authority to obey. If the moral standards and claims of God have been increasingly recognized in the life, then the inadequacy of the parental authority brings no shock to the experience, for the will goes quietly on putting Jesus Christ in control as a guide and corrective for all conduct, and as the closest and never-failing Friend for all exigencies. The lack of experience in life is re-enforced by His wisdom and there is a steady growth in wisdom and judgment.

Contrast, however, the plight of a child of a Christian home who comes to the baffling questions of adult life with no reverence for the authority of its parents because they have never helped it to grow in willing co-operation and with no experience in obeying the still small voice of God in the conscience because His standards never were faced. Right and wrong became blurred because they were ignored. Add to this the positive peril of a self-will that is imperious and uncontrolled, working harm to its possessor as well as to others. Then let such a youth start out in school or business or society, where amidst the confusion of shifting scenes one must see straight and think clearly and find poise, and he is about as safe as a toddler would be on a crowded avenue with no strong one by its side to guide and no wisdom within.

There are hundreds of boys and girls in American Christian homes that are being turned out into adult life thus handicapped. They have no rudder or pilot, no clear-cut standards that line up with the life of Jesus Christ, they are headstrong and impetuous with all the new powers of their adolescence, they are faced by sinister realism and by every possible moral problem, and yet parents and friends refuse to believe that disaster can come to *their* children. Any one who works closely with the youth of to-day knows the result.

Many of those who come from Christian homes fare worse than those from homes where there has been no pretense of Christian upbringing, because when such young people meet disaster they do not turn to Christianity with any hope of finding a guide, because past experience with religion has not commanded their respect; to the non-Christian it may come as a new untried cure for sin. It is a pity that sooner or later, even far along in life, people have to go back and learn the lessons that they should have known as children. Even at the price of fierce struggle these people have to be helped to yield their wills to God and begin to build up a life of obedience. The seeming necessity for the intensities of religious "revivals" is due very largely to the numbers of people who have always lived inwardly rebellious toward God and man, untouched by the ordinary normal teaching of the church.

When we realize that this is often the secret of the lax moral standards and superficial religious life of so many people to-day, we ought to bend all effort toward helping to supplement the lack of religious training in the home with the wisest kind of personal help and influence. We need to understand the particular situation in the life of the average boy and girl in their "'teens" and meet them with a sympathy and personal help that will be real and adequate for their need, so that as soon as possible by their own choice they may put Jesus Christ in full control in their life and conduct and begin to obey Him in everything, cost what it may, entering thus into a normal Christian experience. When they do this, as they see wherein they have been handicapped in the past, they will begin to cooperate intelligently with God in their personal development.

The one daily question of the heart then becomes this: "How can I meet the situations in this day in the spirit of Jesus Christ; what does He want me to do to-day?" So we ought to go on from strength to strength in spite of the stumblings of inexperience and the wrestling with new problems. The Spirit of God guides us into all the truth until we come into our highest self-realization, achieved by the repeated "clash of wills" and co-operation with the revelations of truth that come to us from those in other social groups who, too, are reflecting some part of God's universal truth that we need for our own completeness. Then the relation of the individual Christian to the social group becomes like the relation of the bits of colored glass to the design of a great cathedral window. Each comes to its highest perfection as each is a perfect medium for the glory of the sun, and as each blends with and adds to the beauty of the other bits. In this way alone can the great design and purpose of the artist shine forth.

BIBLE STUDY VI

Entering into the Kingdom

I. *Two types of people who enter.*

(1) Read Matt. 13 : 44. Some people make sudden discoveries of God. They are like the man who stumbled on the treasure unawares and was willing to give up everything he possessed in order to have it. The treasure was revealed by the unexpected turn of circumstances.

What are some of the life experiences which uncover the great treasure in God? See Psalm 119 : 71. Does all sorrow have this effect? If not, why not? Do we have to wait for such experiences to come in order to persuade others to heed the claims of Christ, or is there any other way we can vivify spiritual truth so as to rivet the attention of our friends? What is likely to be the weakness in the development of a Christian experience when the new life has been one of sudden discovery? What its strong points?

> "Why do I creep along the heavenly way
>   By inches in the garish day?
> Last night when darkest clouds did round me lower,
> I strode whole leagues in one short hour!"
>
> (*Mrs. W. F. Slocum.*)

See Acts 16 : 22–34. Why was fear the dominant element in the life of the jailer? Had his work or training anything to do with this? How was this fear transformed into fearlessness (verses 33, 34)? What reconstruction did it immediately require in the attitude of the jailer toward Paul and Silas in view of his former relation to them? (verse 23). In what ways is the jailer like the man in the parable?

(2) Read Matt. 13 : 45, 46. Other citizens of the kingdom are like this man who had always appreciated and traded in pearls, and at last finds one which is worth his entire collection. The appreciation of the great pearl was developed by a long life of appreciating smaller pearls and seeking the best. When people come into the kingdom through a long process of religious education and growth, what in their experience is likely to be a hindrance to reality? What are the advantages and strong points?

See Acts 16 : 14–15. How was Lydia's habit of reverence and worship of God a preparation for Paul's message? Why did not Paul take it for granted that Lydia had the right spirit and therefore did not need further help? Why are we not as keen about the need of such people as we are of those like the jailer? Why is it important to win the Lydias of the world to the fulness of faith in Christ?

> "The path of the righteous is as the dawning light,
>   That shineth more and more unto the perfect day."
>
> (Prov. 4 : 18.)

II. *Some of the conditions for entrance into the kingdom.*

Read Matt. 18 : 1–4. Here the test is that we "turn, and become as little children" in order to enter. What does it mean to become a little child? How can we develop this filial spirit? In view of the fact that we do not know what even a day may bring forth, it is amazing that we should dare for one moment to be anything but little children with our Father; utterly dependent and willing to be guided; trustful and simple in our relationship with Him.

Read John 3 : 3, 5. How can we meet this condition and know that we are born from above? Read Luke 11 : 13 and John 1 : 12, 13. Here the secret is found in the childlike willingness to receive the gift of the spirit of the new life. See also Heb. 10 : 21, 22. The test of being "born of water" is conditioned by our willingness to be cleansed from an accusing conscience through the redeeming love of the Saviour.

Read Matt. 7 : 21-23 for the third condition of entrance into the kingdom—the doing of our Father's will. Love for God and knowing Him is only possible through obedience; making it our ambition to blend our will with His and keeping His commandments. "He that hath my commandments, and keepeth them, he it is that loveth me: and he that loveth me shall be loved of my Father, and I will love him, and will manifest myself unto him" (John 14 : 21).

CHAPTER VII

THE ONENESS OF SPIRIT, MIND, AND BODY

It has been the glory of the Christian faith that the indwelling Spirit of God redeems and transforms not only the spirit and disposition but also the mind and the body; that all three are necessary for full self-realization. The relation between these three is so precise and subtle that each reacts instantly to the experiences of the other. If the body is weakened the spirit is depressed; if the mind is burdened the muscles and circulation of the body show the effects. Even before the Christian era the proverb runs, "A merry heart maketh a cheerful countenance; but by sorrow of the heart the spirit is broken" (Prov. 15 : 13); and the Psalmist asks: "Why art thou cast down, O my soul? And why art thou disquieted within me? Hope thou in God; for I shall yet praise him, who is the help of my countenance, and my God" (Psalm 42 : 11).

It follows, therefore, that if we try to help people to find their centre in God we must take into account not only their spirits but their minds and bodies; for the attitude of the spirit may be a reaction from some mental bias or bodily weakness. These inhibiting causes must be dealt with before the spirit can be set free. Many of the modern vagaries and faddish religious sects have held the popular ear because for so many years the full Christian message of the intimate union of body, mind, and spirit was overlooked. Most of the modern "isms" have come as a natural reaction from the materialistic emphasis of the science of medicine which ignored for so long the relation of mind and spirit to the needs of the body. The reaction has gone to the other extreme, as most reactions do, and preaches the dominance of mind and spirit while it ignores or deplores the body. Both the former materialism of medicine and the spiritual philosophy of the modern cults are inadequate and partial. We will soon have the sense to voice our desires in those reassuring old-time words of Paul: "The God of peace himself sanctify you wholly; and may your spirit and soul (mind) and body be preserved entire, without blame at the coming of our Lord Jesus Christ. Faithful is he that calleth you, who will also do it" (I Thess. 5 : 23, 24).

In tracing the connection between Christian character and bodily states those graphic sentences of Doctor King's may well be emphasized: "The centre of character is self-control. The centre of self-control is will. The centre of will is attention. Now, what has all this to do with the body? Just this. . . . It takes nervous energy to attend; and the supreme condition, therefore, of power of attention, so far as the body is concerned, is surplus nervous energy" (King, *Personal and Ideal Elements in Education*, page 242). We all know only too well the truth of this in our daily experience. The necessity, then, of increasing our surplus nervous energy becomes a sacred obligation which we owe to God if we are honest in asking Him for help in spiritual growth.

A young teacher indulged herself in the excitement of late-hour festivities so that she could not sleep. Then she went to her school with nerves all on edge, so that the slightest incident called forth irritation. Before noon she had lost the respect of all around her for her Christian character. Her margin of nervous energy was too slender to allow her to take liberties with it for even one night. The strain of life is so great that even with a maximum of nervous energy one cannot afford to be a spendthrift. When we form the habit of bringing the needs of every part of our threefold life to God for guidance and control it will be easier to live a proportioned life that will have steadiness and power.

Our margin of nervous energy not only reacts on our disposition but on our mental perceptions. Many cases of mental fog and bewilderment concerning belief in God are a direct result of ignoring bodily needs. A brilliant university student was reported to be in a state of extreme mental tenseness because she could not believe in God, and no intellectual evidence seemed reasonable. A number of people had argued and tried to convince her to no effect. A friend who suspected the real truth took her away for a week-end to sleep long hours, refusing to discuss religion with her. On going back to the university she said shamefacedly: "How could I ever have been such a fool! Of course, I know there is a God. I was too tired to think." It takes the correlation of every part of our being to furnish the perfect instrument on which the Spirit of God can play and reveal Himself.

Sometimes we are caught in the continuity of what seems like "a vicious circle" between spirit, mind, and body. The sins of the spirit depress the mind and rob the body of vitality. This weakened body in turn shackles the spirit so that it yields more easily to sin again, and thus, unless victorious spiritual forces are released to correct such inhibitions, an endless chain of cause and effect is forged.

Chief among these inhibitions is the spirit of *fear*. It is the chronic state of all those who have not an intimate filial relation to the God and Father revealed by Jesus Christ. It is not the will of God that any of His children should be slaves of fear. The Psalmist voices this in his experience: "I sought the Lord and he heard me and delivered me from *all my fears*" (Psalm 34 : 4). The words of Jesus bring the same reassurance: "My peace I give unto you; not as the world giveth give I unto you. Let not your heart be troubled, *neither let it be fearful*" (John 14 : 27). Again Paul confirms this when he says: "For ye have not received the spirit of bondage again to fear; but ye have received the spirit of adoption" (Romans 8 : 15). And yet in spite of this teaching, which is the very heart of the gospel, there are comparatively few whose spirits are not in some kind of bondage to fear. They bear the marks of it in their minds and bodies because they do not accept the deliverance that God provides.

At some time or other every one experiences fear as a result of committing some personal sin. "I heard thy voice and was afraid," falters Adam after he has sinned, and thus he words the universal experience of the race. The fear that comes on the heels of sin saddles the mind with a guilty load and causes the body sleepless hours, takes away buoyant joy, and appetite for food, brings on a restless feverishness or a depressing chill, if, indeed, it does not leave deeper marks on the body. The only sure deliverance comes when we fulfil the condition of owning to our sin and confess it to God and to the one we may have wronged, thus finding the reality of forgiveness in the restoration of the relationships that had been estranged. There are many people who will never be well physically or poised mentally until they deliver their spirits from fear by the confession of their haunting sin.

Again, the spirit of fear may come from the uncertainties in life and circumstances which weight the mind with worry, and is the direct cause of many bodily diseases. We cannot be free spirits until we are delivered from this fear. The secret of deliverance is found, first, in facing the actual truth and cause of the worry, looking at it steadily. Trying to forget worry will not cure it. We must be brave enough to look at the cause honestly, and see how much of it is pure imagination or inference from insufficient data and how serious the actual situation is. When we have detached the real from the imagined burden, we should then ask ourselves whether we have it in our power to change conditions. If we have we must plan quietly to alter them; if we find conditions are beyond our wisdom or control then we must go to God in childlike trust, realizing that nothing is too difficult for Him, give the burden into His keeping, and come away with a relieved heart. Professor James says: "The sovereign cure for worry is religious faith." If our religion does not help us in these matters, if it does not change us, then it would be well for us to seek anew our living heavenly Father.

It is the prayer of faith and trust that sets in motion life-giving forces that bring new vitality to body, mind, and spirit. In order to have a permanent trust, communion with God must be developed not alone by spasmodic pleadings when under great mental stress, but by the daily habit of prayer. It becomes easy to trust God with great anxieties when we have learned to trust Him with small troubles. Doctor Hyslop, superintendent of the Bethlehem Royal Hospital in London, writes: "As an alienist and one whose life has been concerned with the sufferings of the mind, I would state that of all hygienic measures to counteract disturbed sleep, depressed spirits, and all the miserable sequels of a distressed mind, I would undoubtedly give the first place to the simple habit of prayer—such a habit does more to calm the spirit and strengthen the soul to overcome incidental emotionalism than any other therapeutic agent known to me."

The spirit of fear is also caused by insincerity which flies under false colors and sets up false standards. So many lack courage to be themselves and are led on to pretend to be what they are not. This results in mental tenseness and physical fatigue that often ends in nervous prostration. It may be insincerity in false standards of living or the strain of keeping up with what that hypothetical "they" will expect. It may be insincerity in personal relationships in which we are merely posing. Peace and poise can only come by a decision of the will to be genuine and truthful and self-respecting whatever the cost. It means that we speak truth not only in our hearts to God but also in our relations to others. Health and peace have come to many when they have turned away from sham and quietly accepted their limitations in simplicity and honesty.

But it is not alone fear that inhibits the spirit; often it is self-will. This reacts on the mind in irritability and on the body in nervousness. The self-will may be hidden from view because people are so conscious of the mental and bodily effects that they do not realize the cause; but its ear-marks are plainly seen in unwillingness to let others do what they choose and in a constant effort to control the cosmos. One hears such people say: "That woman will drive me crazy," or "I am so nervous I can't stand it," etc. Now, as a matter of fact, they are not likely to go "crazy" or be unable to "stand" things, but they will never get spiritual poise and peace with God until they accept the universe and the people in it as they are, and grant to others the same freedom of action and individuality that they expect for themselves. Such people need a new perspective in which they themselves are small and God's world and all its varied personalities are large. There is nothing that so reduces one's temperature and lowers the nervous pressure as concentrating the mind on the mighty God, and so finding the quietness of a yielded will that is sure that "God's completeness flows around our incompleteness, round our restlessness His rest." *

There is yet one more inhibition on the life of the spirit: it is the spirit of selfishness that reacts on the mind in brooding over slights or neglects and that inevitably generates anger and jealousy with all their serious physical effects. Self-centredness is responsible for many functional diseases and a life is never free for service until this root of trouble is removed. The only remedy is the deliberate denial to self of the right to reign in the heart and the placing of Jesus Christ on the throne

* Mrs. E. B. Browning

of the life, giving Him *in all things* the foremost place. It is only as we face the ugly fact that the jealous love of self always involves hatred of others and cuts us off from the possibility of the relationships of love that we see our need for a Redeemer who can save us from ourselves. "He died for all that they who live should no longer live unto themselves but unto him who for their sakes died and rose again" (II Cor. 5 : 15). It is the gateway into full self-realization, for as we "lose our life" in God we discover in truth that "we find it."

BIBLE STUDY VII

A Full Redemption

I. *The centre of control.*

Read Prov. 4 : 23; Jer. 17 : 9; Eph. 3 : 17, 1st clause; I Cor. 6 : 18, 20; Romans 12 : 1, 2. The human spirit, mind, and body dwell together in harmony only when the spirit or *heart* is in control; and yet the heart cannot control itself. It in turn must be controlled by the Spirit of God. When the body is presented to God as a living sanctuary where He may dwell in full control, the human spirit is then cleansed, steadied, and reenforced for the guidance of the mind and body. See II Cor. 7 : 1.

II. *The sympathetic relation between spirit, mind, and body.*

See Psalm 32 : 1-6. Note the physical effects of the unconfessed sin of the spirit. Read Psalm 77 : 3, 4; Prov. 15 : 13, 30. In what other ways have you traced the interrelation in your own experience? How does the state of the heart show itself in the muscles of the face? in the circulation? in the vitality of the nervous system?

"Of the bodie soul its form doth take
For soul is form and doth the bodie make."
(Spenser.)

III. *The ideal for the Christian.*

I Thess. 5 : 23, 24. If this is the goal, what will be our attitude toward the details of daily living? See I Cor. 10 : 31; II Cor. 5 : 15; II Cor. 10 : 5. If we believed that our spirit, mind, and body were of equal importance in the sight of God, how would this change our ideas about what should be called sacred? What importance did Jesus attach to the healing of the body as well as the heart in his work? Matt. 4 : 23, 24.

IV. *Overcoming the inhibition of fear.*

Read II Tim. 1 : 7; Isaiah 41 : 10, 13; Isaiah 43 : 1. The deliverance from the spirit of fear is the privilege of every Christian. Psalm 34 : 4 ought to be true of every one of us. If we truly believe that God makes our hearts His dwelling-place we ought to find relief from the physical and mental fears in our daily experiences: (*a*) *From the fear of enemies*, Psalm 3 : 4-6. If David could utter these words of quiet trust when fleeing from Absalom, how much more ought we to be able to trust the words of Jesus Christ in John 14 : 27. (b) *From the fear of solitude,* Psalm 4 : 8, using the word "alone" in its marginal rendering "in solitude." (c) *From the fear of future want,* Matt. 6 : 25–34. (d) *From the fear of death,* Psalm 23 : 4; John 14 : 1–3; John 11 : 25. (e) *From the fear of separation from God because of sin,* I John 1 : 7–9; John 8 : 34–36; Matt. 11 : 28, 29.

V. *The transformation of the body because of God's indwelling.*

Read Ex. 34 : 29; Psalm 34 : 5 (in the revised version); Daniel 12 : 3. These words are confirmed by the teaching of our Lord. Note the similarity in the description of Jesus on the Mount of Transfiguration, Matt. 17 : 2, and His description of what the righteous shall be like in the kingdom of their Father. See Matt. 13 : 43. See Acts 6 : 15; also Paul's description in II Cor. 3 : 17, 18, and that of John in I John 3 : 2.

Questions for Study

Why is prayer a means of mental and physical peace? Why would prayer for the body be ineffective unless it were the outcome of a spirit that has been cleansed and whose desires are controlled by God? How do we contradict the desires of our heart through lack of self-discipline in the life of the body? How can the supremacy of the spirit be helped by the body? How is the judgment of the mind affected by a wrong spirit? In view of the purpose that God has for the perfecting of our spirit, mind, and body, why is it that we are so content with a partial redemption that affects only one part of our being?

CHAPTER VIII

REQUISITE CONDITIONS FOR SPIRITUAL COMRADESHIP

We have seen how the mind works naturally according to certain laws and how the development of the Christian life itself follows the natural sequence of cause and effect. In this chapter we shall discuss some of the general principles that every Christian would do well to heed when confronted by an opportunity of coming near to the life of another who needs spiritual help. These principles follow the natural laws of relationship that are dictated by common sense, courtesy, and an appreciation of the sacredness of our trust.

(1) *Always begin at the natural point of contact, starting with what is mutually accepted and known.* Usually the points of agreement in faith will be the stepping-stones to the point yet to be attained in order that full faith and light may come. The inductive method is as useful in matters of religion as in science. It is never wise to begin with an argument in which each person is on an opposite side of a controverted question. It only ends in a mental fencing-match and there can be no real comradeship in it. The way of faith is a path on which one goes without knowing all that is to come, revealing itself slowly as one sure step after another is taken. For example, a person may start out saying, "I do not believe Jesus is the Son of God," and may want to debate the matter. A wise friend will reply: "Well, if He is not that to you, what do you believe Him to be?" The reply may be: "He is the great specialist in character who knew more about what God is like than any other teacher." If that is the point of beginning, be content with that and lead one on to see that if He is the great specialist in character then His teaching is the most trustworthy and should command respect, etc., and then go on to see whether the questioner is willing to begin to follow some of His teaching,

and take literally the challenge, "If any man willeth to do his will, he shall know of the teaching, whether it be of God, or whether I speak from myself" (John 7 : 17). If the challenge can be honestly met then begin to examine some of the teachings that show the unmistakable will of God and begin to apply them unflinchingly to ordinary daily situations. God never fails to lead a spirit out into His truth if this test is made. In other words, we must begin at the exact point in experience where we find people in full agreement and go on with them from step to step, instead of trying to get them to acquiesce in what we see clearly. There is nothing that will so test the honesty of the one who is seeking light as the test that comes from applying at once the light he has as a means of getting more. We must go no faster than we can carry people with us. We shall find that God has not left Himself without a witness in each heart and if we begin at that point in all sincerity, more light will come.

(2) *The natural temperament of the individual will largely determine the method of approach.* Each person must be studied as an individual to whom we must specially adapt ourselves. Our success in this will naturally depend upon our sensitiveness and our powers of observation. There are some of us who seem able to appreciate only one kind of temperament and are not able to understand other kinds. The only way we can gain this knowledge is by studying sympathetically the temperaments of our different friends. Try to discover their especially strong and weak points, their tastes and habits of life—the things they dislike and their mental bias, the way they work and the dominant characteristics of each. Soon by making a comparative study of many of the same temperament we grow instinctively to know what they will like, what parts of the message of Christ will appeal most to them, and what will stir their antagonism. It is a lifelong study, this knowing people; and with all our care and eagerness to help we make big mistakes. It will help us much if we study the very human relations of Jesus Christ and men like Paul, and see how wisely and tactfully they dealt with the different natures of their friends. Love and sympathy are great allies in this. When people recognize these qualities in our hearts they are won, even though their personal peculiarities are not at that time fully understood by us. Surely we would have no right to try to help without a sincere sym-

pathy for different kinds of people and the love of Christ in our hearts.

(3) *It is safe to infer that the real need is usually deeper than the conscious difficulty.* In spiritual diseases as well as in physical illness the real symptoms are often not the apparent ones but are likely to result from a hidden cause. Therefore we should not take obvious difficulties too seriously at first. It is usually true in life that we are more conscious of the effects than we are of the causes. Many people wonder why, for example, they are not conscious of God's presence in prayer and why they seem unable to pray. It takes a mature Christian to sit down and discover through self-examination that there has been some forgotten sin or some unchristian disposition of heart that has hidden the face of God and broken the communion; and that when that is made right the continuity of the prayer life is restored. Similarly, the apparent difficulty may be some failure to win a victory over some habit, although the real cause may be some failure to have faith in God's power, or some neglect in the education of the will. A college girl once confided in a friend that her great spiritual trouble was a lack of reality—that God had seemed for a year or more millions of miles away. In the end she was led to seek the cause in the fact that she had been so angry with her brother over some family matter that she had not written to him for many months. As soon as she dealt with that hard heart of hers and wrote a letter of reconciliation, the sense of God's presence came back to her and as she put it: "It seems as though I would burst with joy—God is so near to me." In the same way one may scoff at Bible study as uninteresting when the real source of trouble is an insincere mind which is not willing to take time for the Christian life, or an unwillingness to meet the moral challenge of the teachings of Jesus Christ.

(4) *Personal conversation should never be carried on with any one in the presence of others. Be sure always to respect personal reserve.* It is only the natural, spontaneous expression of one heart to another that one has a right to know. It seems unnecessary to remind ourselves to be courteous and thoughtful of others; yet we have only to look back into our own experiences to the times when we have been embarrassed by the thoughtlessness of well-meaning people to appreciate the value of this suggestion. There is nothing more harmful than the officious

intrusion into the sanctity of another person's inner life with God and no motive can justify it. We may draw near to another, but we may never intrude. Most of us will appreciate the discerning words of Drummond in his comment on some of the religious workers of the past: "They were most of them wanting in that delicacy of handling which makes analysis effective instead of insulting." The root meaning of the word tact suggests sensitiveness of touch; the kind that *feels* and *senses* situations and discerns the view-point of the other person. Respect for personality and the sacredness of the inner life will keep one free from the clumsy mistakes that are so often made. There is a mystic circle drawn around the personality of every one and no one may step over it without a personal invitation, and without that spontaneous opening of the door whose latch is on the inside. If we have ever been counted worthy to enter the portal we dare not betray that trust by becoming vandals instead of tried friends.

(5) *The greatest helpfulness is only possible when we identify ourselves with the needs of others in the sympathy that speaks of "our needs" instead of "your needs."* It behooves us all to be humble. Any insincerity that shows itself in an "I am holier than thou" attitude shows that we ourselves need to see ourselves as we are in God's presence. It is God's plan that people should learn to know Him through the might of His power working out our transformation; so that all may see what a wonder-working God we have. Paul is continually encouraging us in spiritual growth by referring to the change that has been wrought in him. He glories in the fact that "we have this treasure in a fragile vessel of clay, in order that the surpassing greatness of the power may be seen to belong to God, and not to originate in us" (II Cor. 4 : 7, Weymouth). It is the simple way in which we bear witness to what God has done in us and for us that makes others want to know Him too. This quiet owning up to the way God has helped us never repels; and this spirit is never guilty of intrusion. In fact it binds us to one another with a tie that calls out an answering response, and a desire to share the same experience. There is much wise psychology back of this too. The mind instinctively tends to react and resist in self-defense when facing a direct attack; whereas it is relaxed and off its guard when it is merely the observer of what is going on in another mind. The will is thus relaxed and is

ready for a redirection of effort. It often yields more easily to reaction than to direct pressure—and we shall often be surprised at the moral initiative that is shown at such a time. Every bit of spontaneous desire that comes from the heart of the one we would help will take that person a long way in finding the power of God for himself.

(6) *Whatever is said in counsel should be in harmony with the truth of God rather than the statement of a mere personal opinion.* It is not the harmonizing of one human opinion with another than can help a person to know God, but the reasonableness of faith in His word that brings peace and trust. It makes little difference to another what I think, but it matters much if I can bear faithful witness to the truth of the teaching of Jesus Christ and the way it has worked in my life. It is so easy to sway the life of another by our convictions, especially if that person is bound to us by ties of affection and trust; therefore we must be scrupulous in our care that our convictions are those of Jesus Christ so that they will have permanent value and continue to hold the heart long after we have been taken away from a place of influence. Our words have more weight if we can say: "These are not my words but the explicit teaching of Jesus Christ and He must be right." In this way one has a double appeal; the appeal of one's personal influence, and the appeal of the moral authority of God. This brings full confidence and rest. This does not mean that we are to go around firing Bible verses at people, quoting them as mottoes or preachments. No, the word must become flesh and be incarnated in our life so that as we speak out of our experience, our hearts will be confirming the truth of the word we are teaching. We really possess only as much of God's word as has become part of the fibre of our being.

(7) *Never override the will of the individual.* The temptation often comes to use personal influence and the intensity of desire for another's good to compel a premature decision of the will. Such insidious allurements must be steadfastly resisted. Sooner or later the person so influenced will see that an unfair advantage has been taken at a moment of weakness and a bitter reaction is likely to occur. It is especially easy for an older or more experienced person to bring the pressure of personal influence to bear on younger people. It is only natural for some of us to fall into this temptation through our very

eagerness to help those who are stumbling along in the beginnings of a Christian life. Children are often sinned against in this way, and there are many young people who have been driven away by the overzealous influence of friends who used methods that caused the will to stiffen in opposition to the Christian life. There are others who yielded to the pressure of a masterful personality, but have never developed strength of character and an independent personal relationship with Jesus Christ. We are responsible not only for the people we win by our message, but for the people we drive away, especially when they turn away because we have intruded on the sacred rights of their personalities.

(8) *Human help can only be given by clearing away mental difficulties, pressing the claims of Christ on the life, and the necessity for living not unto self but unto Him.* The real battle with the will must be entered into by a person alone with God, where God does His own pleading and we can help only through intercession. In all earnestness, though, we must inspire the individual to face the lonely struggle with a determined heart and do conclusive thinking, for as Maltbie Babcock once pointed out: "To wish and not to will is spiritual collapse, a house on the sand." Weeks, months, and years may pass before we see the full answer to our prayer. After ten years of refusal to yield to the claims of Christ, a college woman said to the friend who had prayed for her all that time: "Don't ever give any one up. Your patience and unwavering confidence kept me discontented all these years and brought me to Christ."

(9) *Let us guard sacredly all confidences intrusted to our keeping.* Be the most loyal, trustworthy friend and let no lurking desire for vainglory or success as a Christian worker tempt us to use that which has been deposited with us as messengers of God. This is merely the etiquette of loyal friendship. All personal self-revelation is made in the sweet liberty and seclusion of trust and loyalty and one may not betray that confidence without shattering the very ideal that made it possible.

BIBLE STUDY VIII
Christian Comradeship

I. *The promise.*

Read Matt. 18 : 19, 20. These words of our Lord were spoken in the midst of His teaching about forgiveness and the importance of winning back a brother who had forfeited comradeship through a sin against his friend. The words of the promise to the two who agree indicate a power in spiritual fellowship beyond what we think. The spirit that makes us one with God makes us one with others, and the nearer we are to Him the nearer we are to one another. Jesus teaches us that oneness with others is so important that we must do all in our power to restore broken relationships, and that He cares so much that the two or three should be in spiritual fellowship that He is always there in their midst. What is it that usually makes it hard to carry out this teaching? In what ways do we grow spiritually if we follow it?

II. *The illustration.*

Read Luke 24 : 13–25. In this story of the two disciples who were sharing their common convictions and questions, we find Jesus drawing near and walking along with them, according to His promise, although they did not at first recognize Him. Comradeship in spiritual life is necessary for a fuller revelation of God. When we are one with God and one with His children the circuit is complete. The relationship between God and my life is only complete when I am one with another life and say "*Our* Father." In like manner my relation with the life of another is only complete when God is included in it. The comradeship of the two disciples brought unexpected results. (*a*) The immediate presence of Jesus Christ caused their hearts to "burn within" them, verse 32. (*b*) The meaning of their experiences and relationship to Christ was made plain to their illumined hearts, verse 27. (*c*) Their eyes were opened so that they knew Him, verse 31.

Notice the exquisite delicacy of our Lord in waiting for the invitation to "abide" with His disciples. See verse 28. "He made as though he would go further, and they constrained him, saying, Abide with us." He purposed to reveal Himself but waited for their whole-hearted willingness to take Him into the intimacy of their fellowship.

III. *Some general principles.*

(1) In all spiritual comradeship take into account the truth that is already accepted by the one whom we would help. Read Acts 26 : 2–3, 25–27. Note the tact with which Paul takes for granted that Agrippa has done some thinking and is not unfamiliar with his message. He secures the king's intellectual co-operation at the outset. What quality enables us to adapt ourselves to others and understand their point of view?

Read Luke 10 : 25–28. Here Jesus calls out in the lawyer what he already knows until he stands self-judged. The truth to which one is already committed in belief must be lived out before one can be trusted with new truth. How much of truth about God can we usually take for granted in dealing with the average person? What is the advantage of getting them to state it?

(2) We need to reverence human personality wherever we find it. Read Acts 10 : 25–29. In what ways do we need to learn to-day the lesson Peter learned about Cornelius? How big is our world of human sympathies? How many nationalities do we accept as comrades? How many different social types of our own nationality do we treat as brothers?

Read Matt. 18 : 10 and John 4 : 27. What is the limit of our real sympathy? Does it extend to *every* little one who is a child of our Father? If not, why not? How far are we inhibited by the conventional standards of other people from sympathizing with social types different from our own? See Matt. 11 : 19 and Matt. 9 : 11, 12. Do we let the position of other people affect our interest in their spiritual welfare? Are we as interested in obscure people as in those of social position?

(3) We must take into account the time element in growing characters. Read Mark 4 : 26–28. Character-making is a process involving both hope and discouragement. Why are we so impatient and ungenerous toward young Christians? What is a cure for this? On what should we base our comradeship with them? When we look at others we are tempted to see only the points where they come short of us. If we look at Christ we then see where we come short of Him and this begets in us a sympathy for others who come short. At this point real comradeship is possible, for it must be based on an understanding sympathy.

CHAPTER IX

RELEASING SPIRITUAL ENERGY

We have been discerning the natural ways in which our minds react instinctively toward religious influences, and we have come to know some secrets of failure and success in working with people. There yet remains one factor in success without which all skill in dealing rationally with the mind counts for little. It concerns the releasing of spiritual energy, the linking of human strength with the infinite strength of the living God. The great tasks facing humanity demand more than human power to accomplish them. This is because God as Solomon said, "hath set eternity in their heart" (Eccles. 3 : 11) and what we do here in this fleeting life has a significance in the life to come. Therefore we dare not attempt our work with human strength alone; we must claim our privilege as children of God of opening ourselves consciously to His influence, that His power may flow through us.

It is this art of opening ourselves consciously to God's influence and helping our friends to do it that brings about the miracle of all time; that our God who dwells "in the high and holy place" enters in to dwell also "with him that is of a humble and contrite heart." As naturally as the oxygen we breathe into our lungs purifies our blood, so will God transform the life that is open to Him. There are two ways in which God can gain access to a heart: either by the direct response of a person in answer to His voice, or by the response of that heart to some human friend in whom He is living in power. There are many people whose hearts are closed to the great Friend but open to their human friends. To such the flesh is more real than the spirit and their human relationships are, for practical purposes, nearer and dearer than their kinship with God. Therefore God must use the voice of some friend to whom their hearts are open until under the persuasion of that friend they open their hearts directly to God and become His children in spirit and fellowship as well as His by creation. When we realize that God in His infinite eagerness to speak to His children has no other approach to many people than through a human friend, then we will begin to see the sin of thwarting, consciously, God's purposes toward our friend and we will be willing to let Him use us. This will impel us to turn to intercessory prayer as a great means of freeing the energy of God in the life of a friend.

It is the conviction of all those who have had largest experience in Christian service that the practice of intercessory prayer has been an essential factor to success. We are all familiar with the habit of prayer as it relates to our personal needs and to the worship of God; but an honest scrutiny is likely to show that the ministry of intercession has a small place in the daily life. This would not continue to be true if we would give ourselves to a study of this most important subject, the neglect of which is responsible for so much ineffective Christian living.

It is possible to do a human work with a human power but it is impossible to do a superhuman work without superhuman power. The indwelling of the Spirit of Christ in the life of an individual, cleansing, transforming, and energizing that life by the imparting of a divine life, is indeed a miracle wrought by God. We are intrusted with the power of intercessory prayer that we may connect ourselves with the Divine energy and co-operate with God in applying it to the life of the individual. Our responsibility for this is all the greater when we remember that our Lord not only gave long hours to intercession but called his disciples to it as a method of spiritual achievement.

It is not our purpose to discuss the philosophy of prayer in this chapter. The Bibliography at the end includes books that deal with that fully. It is sufficient that we keep in mind the conclusion that Professor James reports after his exhaustive study of religious experiences when he says: "Prayer or inner communion with the spirit thereof—be that spirit 'God' or 'law'—is a process wherein work is really done, and spiritual energy flows in and produces effects, psychological or material, within the phenomenal world" (James's *Varieties of Religious Experience*, p. 485). A correct theory of the philosophy of prayer, however, will not lead one necessarily to pray. It is the convincing evidence of experience that we need. And our experience will bring light just in proportion as we see the underlying principles and use them as a working basis. The immediate aim in this chapter is merely to suggest a few reasons why we should recognize intercessory prayer as necessary in any effort to win disciples and to point out some facts that condition its working.

(1) *Intercessory prayer kills selfishness in us and reveals the sincerity of our interest in people.* In no other way can hidden motives and ambitions be so easily sifted and purified. In it we focus the desires of our heart for the good of another. Our concern for some one else makes us lose sight of ourselves and therefore forces us to serve. The positive desire that God will reveal Himself to the one for whom we pray is in itself a dynamic in us that powerfully expresses itself through our personal influence. There are many of us who will never be able to help another until we desire to do so with all our heart. Unselfishness is the price of power.

(2) *Such prayer quickens love in us.* The yearning for others makes them sacred to us and links us with God in His fatherly eagerness to bless His children. In counting surely upon His love for them we ourselves grow in love. We all know how this principle was urged by Christ when He made it possible for us to obey the command "Love your enemies" by adding another to it: "Pray for them that persecute you." Love is the power that draws one to God and we too can only help in drawing others to Him as we love.

(3) *We need to use intercession also to be made sensitive and susceptible to the needs of others.* In the light of God's presence we see things in true perspective and form right judgments. We see what others may be when God possesses them fully and we carry this ideal for them in our hearts. When our spirits are prepared for service through prayer a spirit of expectancy and watchfulness for God's leadings possesses us. We see our natural opportunities more easily and we have a keener sense of dependence on God.

(4) *Intercessory prayer is the best way to gain a spiritual point of contact with the one we would help.* It saves us from intruding. If we are led to pray intensely for some one else we may expect that God will create in that other heart a sense of need. As we draw near that one our prepared spirit will invite trust and confidence and before we know it we will find our-

selves speaking out of the abundance of our heart. We have a right to expect that God will bring about natural opportunities for personal help if we are ready for them and alert to use them. We probably have many more direct chances to talk with others about God than we suspect. They are passed by because through lack of intercession our hearts were not eager and quick to see. We ought to deal reverently with the thoughts of others that flitter into our minds. Perhaps when we know the laws of the spiritual world better we will find that these promptings are given us by the Spirit of God to call us to prayer because He desires to use us to help these friends in some way. They may, at that very moment, be needing us. It was when Peter was in prayer that he was prepared by a vision to respond to the need of Cornelius, whose messengers were already nearing his door. (Acts 10 : 9–17.) If we believe that God can touch a heart at all we must believe that He can bring the heart that needs Him into relation with some one who can give that help.

Intercession is not an effort to overcome any reluctance of God to help those who need Him, for He is ever yearning to reveal Himself to His children. Intercession is not importunate asking, but the whole-hearted co-operation of mind and spirit in the purpose to be a channel of life and power. It is the sympathetic partnership which releases a divine force operating through natural laws. We must not forget the fact that "we love because God first loved us."

When we study prayer as a working force we will come to see that it is released only on certain conditions:

(1) *Intercession demands the subordination of all desires to the will of God.* The spirit of Christ in Gethsemane must ever be ours. "Father, all things are possible unto thee: howbeit not what I will but what thou wilt" (Mark 14 : 36). Do not dictate times or terms to God. Many prayers cannot be answered until certain experiences have been worked out in the life of the one for whom we pray. Sometimes God means to give "beyond what we ask or think," and to do this requires time. George Matheson, in commenting on apparently unanswered prayers, says: "There are some prayers which are followed by a divine silence because we are not yet ripe for all we have asked; there are others which are so followed because we are ripe for more. We do not always know the full strength

of our own capacity; we have to be prepared for receiving greater blessings than we ever dreamed of. We come to the door of the sepulchre and beg with tears the dead body of Jesus. We are answered by silence because we are to get something better—a living Lord."

(2) *A life obedient to the commands of God is necessary if the life-giving power of the Holy Spirit is to be imparted.* "The Holy Spirit," we are told, God hath given "to them that obey him" (Acts 5 : 32). The fact is that our moral life is the source of all prayer. As we are so we pray. All our real desires affect our prayer. We cannot be petty and critical in heart, and yet pray with intense yearning and love for others; we cannot be fretted and full of complaint and utter the prayer of faith. We must first face in God's presence the condition of our heart before we can expect to intercede with power.

(3) *Intercessory prayer for another does not interfere with the free will and choice of the one for whom we pray.* Prayer creates an atmosphere in which it is easier for the Spirit of God to interpret Christ to the human heart. It suggests God to the mind and brings about conditions in which God can especially press his claims. But the response must be voluntary and spontaneous. "Ye shall seek and find me, when ye shall search for me with all your heart" (Jer. 29 : 13).

(4) *Our Lord places a special value on the united prayer of two or three who are drawn together for the purpose of intercession.* Perhaps it is because two persons are not likely to be drawn together in prayer for a selfish purpose, and so being in accordance with the will of God are able to prevail in prayer. We Christians would do well to study the promise of Matt. 18 : 19, 20 and resolutely meet the condition of united intercession and have fulfilled to us the answer—the presence of Christ, and the granted petition.

"The weary ones had rest, the sick had joy that day
  And wondered how—
The ploughman singing at his work had prayed:
  'God help them now.'

"Alone in foreign lands, they wondered how
  Their feeble words had power—
At home the Christians, two or three had met
  To pray an hour.

> "So we are always wondering, wondering long,
>   Because we do not see
> Some one, unknown, perhaps, and far away,
>   On bended knee."

BIBLE STUDY IX

Prayer

I. *The influence of the example.*

Read Luke 11 : 1–13. What was there about the life of Jesus that led His disciples to say: "Lord, teach us to pray"? The disciples must have felt some great unseen influence at work when they were in the presence of their Master after these times of prayer. It must have made them feel conscious of their spiritual poverty as nothing else. Their desire to be taught was in itself the beginning of the true spirit of prayer and was the spontaneous expression of the heart of a little child which is the condition of entrance into the kingdom of heaven.

II. *The method and underlying principles,* verses 2–4.

What are the marks of its social teaching? What fundamental relationships are mentioned in the prayer? Why are we taught to ask God to measure His forgiveness of us by the measure of our forgiveness of others? If we honestly utter that petition, what will it involve in our life? How does Matt. 18 : 21–35 illustrate this petition? What reason is given in Matt. 5 : 44, 45 (first clause) why we should forgive? How does this principle of forgiving love make us one with the whole world?

III. *The reasonableness of prayer,* verses 5–13.

The argument from human experience. If an unwilling friend will arise in the night and give, is not God better than this grudging friend? (verses 5–10). If a parent gives to a child when it asks, is not God better than a fallible parent? (verses 11, 12). "If ye then know *how*, . . . how much *more* shall your heavenly Father give?" Our belief in prayer is dependent on our belief in our heavenly Father. What kind of a God is your God? Is He merely a Creator or is He also a Father?

> "For the love of God is broader
>   Than the measure of man's mind,
> And the heart of the Eternal
>   Is most wonderfully kind.
> If our love were but more simple
>   We should take Him at His word,
> And our lives would be all sunshine
>   In the sweetness of our Lord."
>   *(Faber.)*

IV. *The relation of our Lord's prayer to the spirit of intercession.*

Can we pray the first three petitions of the Lord's prayer without putting our lives into the answer? Why is intercession for others the highest form of prayer? Intercessory prayer is commanded by Christ and strengthened by His own example. "Pray for them that persecute you" (Matt. 5 : 44), and "The harvest indeed is plenteous, but the laborers are few. Pray ye therefore the Lord of the harvest, that he send forth laborers into his harvest" (Matt. 9 : 37, 38). We cannot turn away lightly from the power of that intercession of Jesus as we read His prayer in the seventeenth chapter of John. In fact, we cannot think of our Lord as detached from this big suffering world of need but as yearning to see its complete redemption; as the writer of the letter to the Hebrews puts it: "He ever liveth to make intercession for us" (Heb. 7 : 25).

It is significant that Luke, in his account of Jesus' teaching concerning prayer, emphasizes the gift of the Holy Spirit in answer to prayer. See Luke 11 : 13. We are told also in Romans 8 : 26 that the "Spirit helpeth our infirmity, for we know not how to pray as we ought; but the Spirit . . . maketh intercession for us" and "he maketh intercession for the saints according to the will of God." It is an unspeakable comfort to know that in this great work of intercession we are not left alone, but are to be guided "into all the truth" by the Spirit and that He is to "teach you all things and bring to your remembrance all that I (Christ) said unto you" (John 14 : 26).

Questions for Thought

How is intercession a discipline in unselfishness? How does it affect the horizon of our life? How does it affect our service for others? Am I prepared to pay the cost of intercessory prayer for those whom God relates to my life? I can do a human service for some one with a human power; I can do a divine service for some one only with divine power. Am I willing to meet the tests in order to have that divine power?

"We shall not have to talk so much to others if we pray more for them. We talk and do not influence, or we influence only for a time, because our lives are not more prayer-full. . . . Talking may be a great snare when it takes the place of prayer—and how easily it does! It is easier to talk with a man than to pray for him—in many cases" (Forbes Robinson's *Letters*, pages 95 and 105).

CHAPTER X

THE PROBLEM OF THE NOMINAL CHRISTIAN

The nominal Christian presents the dreary spectacle of arrested development. One sees many such. The life history of each is ordinarily the same. As children their hearts are sensitive to the call of Jesus and respond gladly. Later, during the years of adolescence, the relationship to God becomes more clearly defined and they gladly acknowledge Christ as Saviour and enter the fellowship of the church. Then usually follows a time of eager devotion and loyalty. The life of such a person seems so vigorous and full of promise. Then with irresistible force the responsibilities, opportunities, temptations, and complex interests of adult life take possession of the untested Christian. At the same time they are likely to go away from home for business or college and are cut off from the inspirations and counsel of trusted, tried friends who have always held them true to the ideal. Then it is that any one of a number of causes weakens the strength of the vital life. Its power, joy, and God-consciousness dwindle and cease to meet the heart's need. Such Christians see the unreality of this inner life and conclude that what was one time a conscious reality of the spiritual life was merely the unthinking enthusiasm of childhood and not possible for the sophisticated adult. They resolve to be honest, at any rate, and not play the part of a hypocrite by clinging to the form when the reality is gone. Little by little church attendance and Christian service are stopped, and they frankly mingle their lives with the motley throng of those whose lives are like that described in the words:

> "I lived for myself, I thought for myself,
> For myself and none beside;
> Just as if Jesus had never lived,
> And as if He had never died."

One who would help in winning back to Christ the sincere loyalty of these nominal Christians must grapple with the causes which lie back of this arrested development. Briefly, the more common of these causes might be summed up in the words—starvation, suffocation, disobedience, and bewilderment.

The process of starving the spiritual life is a simple one. In gradually giving less attention to what are sometimes called "the means of grace" the life inevitably loses its vitality. Before they know it some Christians become thoughtless toward God and their moral responsibilities. They drift away, not through deliberate sin but through neglect. They have become enamoured of distracting pleasures and "follow the crowd" with no sense of moral purpose, and do not even realize the receding of their Christ, who used to be a near Companion. Such people are rarely quickened except by some shock which shatters their day-dreams and brings them face to face with their elemental needs.

One of the blessed uses of suffering is that it keeps us alive. Just as the burn of the finger keeps the child from destroying its hand in a flame, so God uses the earthquakes and fire of our daily experience to keep us from spiritual stupor. Sometimes failure in business, an accident or loss of a friend, or a cruel disappointment are the only means that will lead the nominal Christian to crave God anew. If so, then the friend who would help must stand by in patience and prayer and friendliness waiting for a sense of need in the life of that friend. Then it will be possible to interpret the earthquake and fire as the prelude to that "still small voice" of God who longs to reveal Himself to-day to His children just as He did at that historic moment of Elijah's life. But one need not always wait for these hard experiences to come before help can be given. Often the necessary shock can be given by a straight, true word spoken in love and intense earnestness. One day one of those thoughtless Christians, already in the forties, was telling a Christian friend of her position in a school where, she said, she had come to know well more than nine hundred girls during the years she had been there living with them for nine months of the year. Her friend exclaimed: "Oh, what opportunities you have had for giving them ideals!" "Ideals? Not I," she said gayly. "I merely enjoy their company and do not bother about their morals or manners." Very suddenly her friend turned and said: "I shouldn't like to be in your place—suppose Jesus Christ should come and expect an accounting from you to-morrow! You know I can't get away from those words: 'Every one of us must give an account of himself to God.'" A silence fell between them and they soon parted. Two days later the teacher came to her friend and said: "Please help me to find God—I've thought of nothing night or day but that line you quoted to me—my life has been so empty—and I cannot rest for thinking of the girls I might have helped." It was the revealing fire of God that brought her to a new sense of her responsibility to God and to His children, and the record of the years since have proved what one woman, in whose life God has the foremost place, can do for scores of girls who now look to her as their spiritual mother. And she often writes to her friend in words like these: "I can never cease to thank God that He gave you the courage to 'stab my spirit broad awake.'"

Sometimes, too, we gain the chance to help the nominal Christian to reality in the spiritual life by making sure that we ring true in little things—in some of the very ways where one's genuine sincerity can best be shown. It is generally little things that show up the chasm between the life that is genuine in its loyalty to Christ and the one that is nominal. At a summer resort a girl slipped away each Sunday morning to a neglected little church for the service. Returning one day she met a gay friend who said: "Where have you been?" "Over to the little church beyond the meadow," the girl replied simply. "To that pokey little place on this hot day? You must be frightfully pious!" "Not at all, but I go because I couldn't get through the week without it. It helps to keep me reminded, and I need it." The society friend looked at her curiously and said slowly: "Why, your religion must be actually *real* to you. I wish mine were." Then a natural opening for a friendship started which led the society girl into a renewal of her Christian life which has blessed multitudes through her Christian philanthropy and the application of the principles of Jesus Christ to the social problems of her father's industrial community.

It is comparatively easy to gain opportunities to win back to reality those nominal Christians. One can reckon on a certain susceptibility to spiritual influence, for the chances are with most of them that their consciences are still pricking them occasionally. Crystal sincerity, courage, alertness, and the ringing true in little things will usually develop natural opportunities for personal service beyond all that one could hope.

After the opportunity for honest fellowship has come one must try to restore in the starved Christian the broken habits of the Christian life. Chief among these is secret prayer. Even on days when one does not feel inspired to pray, there is then all the more need to pray. The unvarying daily practice of bowing in the presence of the heavenly Father and opening the heart in stillness that His Spirit may prepare it and steady it for the day's work will surely bring its reward. "Be still and know that I am God."

Closely related to this is the strength that comes from church life and fellowship with other Christians. We owe more of our spiritual fibre to this than is commonly supposed. The study of the moral and religious conditions in pioneer towns where church fellowship is meagre brings out this fact, and vital Christianity dwindles. Close comradeship with those who lightly regard the claims of Jesus Christ usually saps the strength of the Christian. Then, too, the discipline of some bit of daily service for Christ's sake develops moral muscle. The world is so full of need that the true disciple cannot ignore it without suffering loss in those finer qualities of spirit. One of the chief causes of nominalism lies in the fact that Christians have been individualists and lived as though what they did was of no concern to society or as though they had no obligations to the social community. If they once were to begin to get under the burden of the whole community as if it were their own they could not be careless and thoughtless. The steady strain of Christlike service helps to keep one's feet on the earth and brings reality into one's vision. We should do everything in our power to supply the tonic of some definite service to the thoughtless Christian. It will work wonders.

We must also help these friends by lure of some study of the Scriptures that will bring a daily moral challenge to them and compel them to test their life according to the teachings of Jesus. They will find, then, that His words are literally true. "The words that I speak unto you, they are spirit and they are life" (John 6 : 63).

As surely as the life is reconnected with these neglected sources of strength new vigor and reality will come, and it is by these means alone that the more subtle suffocating influences can be overcome. These influences are strong among a class of nominal Christians who could never be called thoughtless;

but they are, nevertheless, a stumbling-block to the progress of the kingdom. They are not irresponsible people; they are those whose standards are blurred and who suffer from spiritual astigmatism.

These people are described by our Lord in the parable of the seed falling into the ground in which there were thorns and briers (Mark 4 : 18, 19). In this He speaks plainly about those who had heard the word but have allowed it to become choked. Three causes are mentioned: first come the "cares of the world." Nothing could be more plausible. "Cares" are a part of a normal adult life and are given for the good of the individual. The wrong comes when nominal Christians allow themselves to be utterly absorbed by these cares. There is no time for God because all time is given to selfish interests. The temptation is so insinuating that the yielding comes almost before one is aware of it. Religion becomes an opiate rather than a stimulant. The student has no time for spiritual things because work is so pressing, the mother must care for her children, and the demands of business press on others. And yet it was to such that Jesus spake the words: "Come unto me all ye that labor and are heavy laden and I will give you rest. Take my yoke upon you and learn of me."

Closely related to "cares" comes the "deceitfulness of riches" —the self-indulgence and love of ease and the desire to sacrifice everything for personal ambitions. And let us note that this is no more true of the rich person who has gained possession of riches than it is of the poor person whose heart is set on the same goal. All these things tend to sap the spiritual vigor, and the spirit is not at leisure from itself to worship the Father and to grow in grace. The spiritual life is only victorious when the Christian, conquering the temptation of riches, uses them to serve higher ends as a means for the larger service for the kingdom.

The third cause of suffocation is described by the phrase "the desires of other things"—the selfish purposes that have crowded out the purpose of living for Christ which they once had. The ambition for popularity, a career, social success, anything that diverts the attention from the supreme end of life and hinders Christ from carrying out His gracious purposes in us.

"The Lord Christ wanted a tongue one day
   To speak a message of cheer
To a heart that was weary and worn and sad,
   And weighed with a mighty fear.
He asked me for mine, but 'twas busy quite
With my own affairs from morn till night.

"The Lord Jesus wanted a hand one day
   To do a loving deed;
He wanted two feet, on an errand for Him
   To run with gladsome speed.
But I had need of my own that day;
To His gentle beseeching I answered, 'Nay!'

"So all that day I used my tongue,
   My hands, and my feet as I chose;
I said some hasty, bitter words
   That hurt one heart, God knows.
I busied my hands with worthless play,
And my wilful feet went a crooked way.

"And the dear Lord Christ—was His work undone
   For lack of a willing heart?
Only through men does He speak to men!
   Dumb must He be apart!
I do not know, but I wish to-day
I had let the Lord Christ have His way."

(Alice J. Nichols.)

The precise counsel that these people need is help in finding a true perspective. They usually want a deeper spiritual life, but seem caught in the mesh of legitimate cares until they become unfruitful in the life of the spirit. To get a true perspective they need first to be led to give God the full control of all the details of their life—to begin to make Him their first confidant and not merely a refuge in an emergency. Instead of making their decisions according to what other people are doing or think it right to do, they need to be helped to look at their daily life of duties, resources, and privileges in the light of the prayer: "Lord, what wilt thou have me to do?" They also need to be shown how to begin to practise the habit of counselling with Him about the daily needs. They will then find a new perspective for their life as they practise the presence of God. In the end there will come a new sense of relative values that will bring liberty and poise and the release of latent power that will drive anxiety, depression, and the fear of nervous prostration from their experience. No witness to the reality of the presence of God could be plainer than to find Him as the centre of control in the lives of busy people who show forth the joy of a full service of God, revealing Him to be their great Friend and not a hard taskmaster.

Another important cause of nominalism remains yet to be stated. It is that subtle paralysis that creeps into the life as a result of unconquered sin. Perhaps it may be that the nominal Christian has failed to understand and use the laws that bring victory over temptation and is discouraged by repeated failures to live true to the heart's purpose. Or the ugliness of sin may be veiled by attractive excuses so that the desire to resist is half-hearted or gone.

The one who would help such imprisoned spirits must understand the seat of the difficulty which finds its cause in an inert will. Such people are naturally weak in will-power and in moral decision of character, or they may be so strong in will that they are stubborn and inhibited by pride from yielding to God's Spirit. If the person is weak in will, a strong friend can legitimately use personal influence to help them to be true to their awakening conscience. The result of squaring oneself with one's conscience will bring a new vigor into life that will help a person another time to do the right on their own volition. An instance of this was found in the life of a girl who had yielded to the temptation to steal a treasured book from a friend's house several years before and had from that time on given up her Christian life. Under the influence of a Christian friend who in ignorance of the cause for her indifference was urging her to renew her Christian life, she said: "Oh, I used to be a real Christian like you, but it has ceased to be real to me since I was fifteen years old." "When did you first lose your sense of God? What caused it?" came the questions. Whereupon, as she told how she had stolen the book, it developed that, although she knew the cause all along, her will had been too weak for years to make the matter right with God and her conscience. The next day, under the influence of her friend, who handed her notepaper and a pen, in her presence she wrote a letter to the one she had wronged confessing her fault and assuring her of the return of the book by the next mail. Her friend went with her to mail the letter in the box and stood by her in faithfulness. The result was that the inertia of years was overcome and God became so real to her that she was from that day able to grow in moral decision of character.

To a stubborn nature the appeal to the will for decision is the line of greatest resistance and is not usually successful. Such people are more easily won through their affections. They will find it easy to do anything for one whom they love. They need to be shown the love of God who yearns now over His disobedient children as in the days of old when He pled with His people: "Have I been a wilderness unto Israel? or a land of thick darkness? Wherefore say my people: 'We are broken loose; we will come no more unto thee.'" They need to see the pathos of a strong nature resisting the gentle Spirit of God, who longs to purify them and lead them back into peace and power. They also need to be appealed to by a challenge to their sense of pride in being honorable with God and facing things squarely and ceasing to be a sham. Slowly but surely this kind of appeal will bring a response from such Christians, and what was one time stubbornness will become a strong will nerved for any task and real spiritual conquest. This type of nominal Christian makes the finest kind of Christian worker when once guided back to a true life.

One more cause of nominalness should be considered. It is that sense of mental bewilderment that exists largely because of an inadequate or fantastic conception of God. The crude religious ideas of childhood may never have been changed. Parents, Sunday-school teachers, and ministers may have taken for granted that the young Christian would have the right conception of God, without intelligent guidance, and so wonder why there is so little interest in the Christian life. Many a student has found that mental integrity forbids further belief in their childish ideas of God and yet has not discovered an honest basis for faith in the conception of God as revealed by Jesus Christ. These intellectual difficulties will be discussed more fully in another chapter, but their relation to the problem of the nominal Christian is often a real one. The sense of bewilderment may often come because of a misunderstanding of the relation of God to the sorrows of life. Here again the true conception of God is warped in that He seems cruel and far away from the distress of His children. Thus it is that bitterness of heart and estrangement from Him creep in.

The experience of the nominal Christian is never a happy one.

> "For, oh, the Master is so fair,
> His smile so sweet to banished men,
> That they who meet it unawares
> Can never rest on earth again."

One can always count upon the memory of past trust and knowledge of God as an ally in trying to help these friends back to Him. They are naturally discontented and restless because they have once known the joys of Christian life. Their potential value to the kingdom of God is great and from them should be recruited scores of ardent workers for Jesus Christ. Like the story of the debtors in the parable, they love much because they have been forgiven much. It is well to devote much prayer and energy to this work, for it is the Christian in name only that is the greatest stumbling-block to unbelievers. Still, God can do to-day what he has been doing for centuries past; He still works transformations through the power of His Spirit.

"I will sprinkle clean water upon you and ye shall be clean: from all your filthiness, and from all your idols, will I cleanse you. . . . And I will multiply you the fruit of the tree, and the increase of the field, that ye shall receive no more the reproach of famine among the nations" (Ezek. 36 : 25-30).

BIBLE STUDY X
The Problem of Arrested Development

Read Luke 8 : 4-15. Four kinds of soil into which the seed of the truth of God falls.

(1) *The wayside*, verses 5, 12. Here the seed cannot take root because the mind has become the common runway for so many ideas and impressions that it is impervious to anything. Therefore the seed is spirited away. See Heb. 3 : 13 for one cause of the hardening process.

What are the chief causes of mental atrophy to-day? Why is superficial, cosmopolitan living such a menace to the growth of the spirit? How can we keep from mental insensibility? Are we responsible for keeping our spirits sensitive? Have I been used to thanking God that things touch me deeply? Is it possible to educate the conscience into a sense of moral responsibility?

(2) *The rocky ground*, verses 6, 13. Here the word is received with joy but withers because there is no root. They "for a *while* believe," but wither under testing. There is great danger if we have a restricted area

in our hearts not subjected to the ploughing of God's Spirit. Having reservations from God is a menace to our future and to our power of retaining even the little life that was a joy to us. We need to let God apply to our hearts the message of Jer. 23 : 29 and Ezek. 36 : 26 and I Peter 1 : 5–7, in which God's truth, God's Spirit, and God's discipline are the means of preparing the ground of the heart for the life of the seed. How far are we responsible for producing nominal Christians by inadequate teaching and preparation of the soil for the planting of the truth? How do we fail people by not ploughing deep? In what ways will our relations with those we would help be different if we have this in mind?

(3) *The seed falling among thorns*, verses 7, 14. The ground is prepared and rich but it needs the weeding and pruning and gardening of God's Spirit; therefore, "as they go on *their* way" the "thorns choke," *i. e.*, cares, riches, and pleasures of this life. Many of them are legitimate interests but used for *our own way*. The secret of failure lies in a lack of purpose and focus of all powers on a life to be lived "no longer unto themselves but unto him" (II Cor. 5 : 15 and Romans 15 : 3). How soon in Christian experience ought this full dedication to come? Is it easier before or after a growing acquaintance with God as a Friend? Ought we to be content with merely helping one to a beginning of acquaintance with Him? What connection has *service* with the development of purpose?

(4) *The seed on the good ground*, verses 8, 15. Here the secret is the *honest* and good heart which holds the truth *fast* and brings forth *fruit* with *patience*. This involves a right attitude of sincerity, will-power, and a vision of the goal that helps one to have patience. Therefore, in any constructive help that we give to nominal Christians we must seek to develop: (*a*) moral sensitiveness, (*b*) a spirit that regards weaknesses and besetting sins as special opportunities for the showing of God's power, (*c*) a purpose to give Jesus Christ the foremost place and to deny self the right to reign, (*d*) honesty and a willingness to let the truth go deep, and patience with oneself in fruit-bearing.

CHAPTER XI

THE APPROACH TO THE NON-CHRISTIAN

A discerning Japanese Christian said recently that one of the surprising peculiarities about Americans was the fact that we used the word Christian as though it were an adjective instead of a noun. It is only too true. We think of non-Christians as living in the Orient, but many of us would shrink from the apparent discourtesy of labelling any of our friends in this country non-Christians. The irresistible influence of Jesus Christ has entered into our whole social fabric, and people unconsciously have taken Christian ideals as the only possible ones for well-bred people, and they conform to their standards outwardly, often from sheer necessity, because the ideals of the world are, after all, the ideals of Jesus Christ. But it is as true to-day as it was in the days of old when it was said: "This people draw near me with their lips but their hearts are far from me" and "As a man thinketh in his heart so is he." The weary-eyed, anxious faces of men and women all about us tell us only too plainly that they have never heard personally the invitation of Christ: "Come unto me, all ye that labor and are heavy laden, and I will give you rest"; or if they *have* heard it they have not accepted it nor found their life in Him as Christians. They are all about us—these non-Christians, unrelated to Jesus Christ, like withered branches that are severed from the vine. The pathos of our American brand of non-Christians lies in the fact that they starve with food in sight while the non-Christians of the Orient starve without food in sight.

When we try to get at the heart of the matter we see that in the case of a non-Christian the habitual attitude of mind and heart is that of unbelief in the message of Jesus Christ and its personal significance. This unbelief may be the inheritance of centuries or it may have crystallized from the experiences of a short lifetime or it may be the mere willingness to go on living without any personal knowledge of God. To such people the story of Jesus Christ as the gift of God to men is merely a beautiful tale to tell children and not a challenge to their adult life. There is no conscious sense of relationship with a heavenly Father; the connection is cut and they are, as Paul says, "without hope and without God in the world."

There are certain causes which lie back of a state of unbelief and which must be dealt with if we are to be of service.

(1) *Simple ignorance of the true character of God as revealed by the life of Jesus Christ is responsible for much unbelief.* If one realized the love of our heavenly Father and the priceless value of our lives in His sight as shown by the sacrificed life of His Son that we might have life through Him, it would not be possible to be unreceiving in heart and mind.

> "Oh, could I tell ye surely would receive it;
> Oh, could I show you what mine eyes have seen;
> How can ye know and how can ye receive it;
> How—till He bringeth you where I have been?"

The only remedy for ignorance is knowledge, and that knowledge comes through the study of the life of Christ in the gospels and the interpretation of that life and its principles in the epistles. Persuade the unbeliever to begin a study of one of the gospels to discover the true nature of the heavenly Father and the teaching of Christ. It may not be willingness but facts that he needs. "The same Lord is Lord of all, and is rich unto all that call upon him. . . . How then shall they call on him in whom they have not believed? and how shall they believe in him whom they have not heard? . . . So belief cometh of hearing, and hearing by the word of Christ" (Romans 10 : 12–17).

(2) *Prejudice is the close friend of ignorance.* Prejudice is ignorance confirmed by some experience. Perhaps, as a child, the non-Christian was taught some crude notion of God that contradicted the instincts of the heart and quenched the desire for God. Or, as often happens, the only zealous Christian one has known may have been some one whose life did not square with the teachings of Christ. There are also many red-blooded non-Christians who have become so as a protest against some barren, anæmic, contracted ideal of life that was set forth as the only model Christian life. They mistake one instance for

a principle and judge by the crudities of discipleship rather than by the teaching of Jesus Christ. Such prejudices are only displaced by other normal experiences that gain control over the affections. We must challenge such people to judge the case for Jesus Christ by going straight to His teachings and forming an honest judgment.

In working with people who have been born in lands under the sway of non-Christian religions, the element of prejudice bulks large. It takes months and years often to overcome it by building up confidence through friendship with them and through the new ideas that are developed by Christian education. It is not easy for one who has been bound by the traditions of many centuries suddenly to become open-minded to new truth. The process is simpler if one can find some common meeting-ground and discover elements in the past inheritance that will form a background for the new teaching. There are certain ethical teachings in every non-Christian religion that parallel certain Christian teachings. These can be taken as a starting-point for fuller revelation.

(3) *A failure to appreciate the true nature of sin is the root of much indifference and unbelief.* Here one is prone to trust to relative values. For example, certain people are accustomed to look on others in whom they see sin and weakness and to say with complacency: "What a pity that they are so weak! I am glad that I have too much self-respect to be like that." And even when looking on some very worthy earnest Christian they rejoice to discover some point of imperfection in which they feel superior to that servant of God. They console themselves with this evidence of discernment on their part while at the same time they fail to realize their own shortcomings.

It is only when they realize that our holy God is a consuming fire, to "prove each man's work of what sort it is" (I Cor. 3 : 13) and that "each one of us shall give an account of himself to God" (Romans 14 : 12) that they are startled into the recognition of a personal responsibility to God that has hitherto been ignored. In this serious meditation it is well to recall Paul's words: "I judge not myself, for I know nothing against myself; yet am I not hereby justified: but he that judgeth me is the Lord" (I Cor. 4 : 4). They can only come again to the teachings of Jesus Christ and let these reveal how great is each one's need and sin. These teachings will also reveal that the greatest sin is that of unbelief and that the most sinful thing one can do is to refuse to let God into one's life. And in realizing this they will begin to be aware of the working of the Holy Spirit who, as Jesus said, "will convict the world of sin, because they believe not on Me" (John 16 : 9).

(4) *A discouragement born of long-continued hopeless conflicts with the limitations, sins, failures, and weaknesses of one's life keeps many in a state of unbelief.* It does not seem possible to them that God can transform the life when they themselves have tried so often and failed. They may have seen his mighty work in the life of another but are confident that these persons possessed more will-power at the start or had less to contend against and thus they could win an easy victory. And unfortunately there is much current teaching which would deceive people into believing that one attains righteousness by the works of the law instead of by the grace of our Lord Jesus Christ. "By grace have ye been saved through faith; and that not of yourselves, it is the gift of God; not of works, that no man should glory" (Eph. 2 : 8, 9).

We must patiently persuade these discouraged, unbelieving persons to give up the struggle and let God do for them what they cannot do for themselves. This involves the yielding of themselves to Him in faith that according to the promise of Christ He will free them from the burden of the unfulfilled requirement of accepted human laws and the moral claims of one's heart, and then indeed He will give rest. "Come unto me all ye that labor and are heavy laden and I will give you rest" (Matt. 11 : 28), "for apart from me ye can do nothing" (John 15 : 5).

(5) *A spirit of fear holds many back from believing the message of Christ.* They are usually persons of integrity of mind who realize that God's claims involve full surrender to His will and purposes and that no half-way position is possible. They also feel the tug of personal ambitions and unbelieving friends and a certain sense of prudence makes them cautious about entering upon a new and untried life where large issues are at stake. It is seemingly far simpler to go on walking alone by sight than to walk with God in faith and to take the risks of full obedience. These persons need to realize the infinite love of the compassionate Christ which casts out fear. They must be led to see that God never takes an unfair advantage of a

life intrusted to Him, but that "he that loseth his life for my [Christ's] sake shall find it" (Matt. 10 : 39).

As soon as the cause that lies back of the unbelief is known one can begin from that starting-point to lead on into faith. A long first step is made when open-mindness is secured. That may come easily or with difficulty according to the temperament of the individual. Comradeship with a broadminded, honest type of Christian may create a new hunger for God; a fresh interpretation of the teaching of Christ or hard experiences may make the heart susceptible to Him. There are probably all about us more open-minded unbelievers than we suspect whose hearts have been prepared through life experience for our interpretation of Christ. For many reasons they are open-minded toward us, and it is our unspeakable privilege to help them to be open-minded toward God. If they can trust us why should we not help them to trust Him? They need a sincere attitude of open-mindedness toward all possible light, and courage to face the cause of the unbelief and to have that cause removed by opening the heart to the influence and teachings of Christ. An honest search for light will bring its own reward. Paul describes this attitude in the words: "Be ye transformed by the renewing of your mind, that ye may prove what is that good and acceptable and perfect will of God" (Romans 12 : 2). It is also so simply stated by Jesus when He says: "Except ye turn and become as little children, ye shall in no wise enter into the kingdom of heaven" (Matt. 18 : 3). By an act of the will we must become teachable if we would know God.

The next step into belief is to centre the attention upon Jesus Christ as the revelation of God to men. It is not Christianity but Christ with whom the individual has first to reckon. It is possible to talk for hours about the principles of Christianity without facing the claims of the personal Christ. The result of all conversation should be an increased God-consciousness, a deepened sense of moral responsibility to a living, personal God, and a growing appreciation of a possible personal relationship with Jesus Christ as the One through whom alone we can live a life in harmony with the purposes of God.

> "Christ, I am Christ's and let that name suffice you;
> Ay, for me, too, He hath greatly sufficed.
> Lo, with no winning words I would entice you;
> Paul has no honor, and no friend but Christ."

Having opened the mind to the teachings of Jesus, we must, with decision of character, resolve to obey all the truth that is made clear to the mind. Faithful obedience to the light already given brings belief and more light. And each person has some light to follow. There is at least one teaching or command of Christ that the mind and conscience own to be reasonable and necessary. Let this be taken literally and obeyed implicitly and light and guidance will come inevitably from this doing of God's will.

In the same way we must help people to begin to pray. Even though the mystery of prayer is not understood and experience in answered prayer has been lacking, yet there is usually a recognition of the holiness, greatness, and infinite Fatherliness of the living God and one must acknowledge this by kneeling before Him in worship. Jesus said: "Pray to thy Father who is in secret, and thy Father who seeth in secret shall recompense thee" (Matt. 6 : 6); and "Ask, and ye shall receive, that your joy may be made full" (John 16 : 24). An honest heart that truly desires to come into a knowledge of the heavenly Father must be willing to take the step of humbling oneself before Him and speaking to the One who, like the father in the parable, has been waiting for the child to come to himself and say in sincerity: "I will arise and go to my father."

In beginning the habit of prayer it is a great help to commit to memory some of the prayer Psalms and make them a personal prayer. Such Psalms as the 51st; 17 : 1–8; 42; 84; 90; 103; 119 : 9–16, 57–64, 73–80, 121–130; 139; 141 are guides for the expression of the heart and teach one how to pray.

We must remember that it is futile to attempt an answer to all questions concerning spiritual realities. The answers will come with growing experience; they are revealed as one goes on. In all our efforts to win others we need to shift the battle from the ground of mere discussion to an attack upon the citadel of the will. The truest help is given when one is shown how to take the next step toward God and the Christian life. A little child learns to walk not by being carried from room to room, but by tottering along with some friendly person near by to lift it to its feet when it stumbles. In the same way one needs the wisdom of God to know when to help and when merely to stand by in prayer and sympathy.

The successive decisions required in taking the steps already suggested prepare the way for a more complete functioning of the will-power. It is difficult to follow honestly up to this point without facing Jesus Christ and the love that made Him willing to pour out His soul unto death—the death of the cross—that we might live. It will be easy then to recognize His right to full authority in the life. There will be a growing desire to place Him on the throne of the heart. The crisis will be on when, in childlike faith by an act of the will, the heart confesses His right and bows to it.

> "Laid on Thine altar, O my Lord divine,
>   Accept my gift this day, for Jesus' sake;
> I have no jewels to adorn Thy shrine,
>   Nor any world-famed sacrifice to make,—
> Just here I bring within my trembling hand
>   This will of mine—a thing that seemeth small,
> And only Thou, dear Lord, canst understand
>   How, when I yield Thee this, I yield mine all!
> Hidden therein, Thy searching eye can see
>   Struggles of passion, visions of delight,
> All that I love, or am, or fain would be,—
>   Deep loves, fond hopes, and longings infinite.
> It hath been wet with tears and dimmed with sighs,
>   Clenched in my grasp, till beauty it hath none.
> Now from Thy footstool, where it vanquished lies,
>   The prayer ascendeth, 'May Thy will be done.'
> Take it, O Father, ere my courage fail;
>   And merge it so in Thine own will that e'en
> If in some desperate hour my cries prevail,
>   And Thou give me my gift, it would have been
> So changed, so purified, so fair have grown,
>   So one with Thee, so filled with peace divine,
> I may not know or feel it as mine own;
>   But, gaining back my will, may find it Thine."

From that time on there come joyful discoveries. Jesus Christ becomes a personal Saviour in whose presence besetting sins shrivel up and disappear. There is also heard a new note of authority in the heart which proclaims this Christ as Master for a new life of worth-while service. He guides into "paths of righteousness for His name's sake" and releases inner latent energies for spiritual conquest. And as the days go on one begins to realize the presence of Christ as a satisfying Friend. His companionship raises the standard of friendships and brings a new sense of values into life. Thus belief and trust in God come naturally. It is the logical result of an experience gained by meeting certain conditions.

> "You ask me why I thought this loving Christ would heed my prayer?
> I knew He died upon the cross for me—I nailed Him there!
> I heard His dying cry—'Father, forgive!'
> I saw Him drink death's cup that I might live:
> My head was bowed upon my breast in shame!
> He called me and in penitence I came.
> He heard my prayer! I cannot tell you how
> Nor when nor where—only I love Him now."

BIBLE STUDY XI
Winning the Non-Christian

I. *The explanation of the non-Christian life.*

See Romans 1 : 18–23. (See the Moffat translation.) The trend downward is natural and easy.
   (1) The truth was suppressed deliberately—although it was all about them in nature (verses 18–20).
   (2) Although people knew God, they did not give Him glory or exalt Him (verse 21).
   (3) They were *unthankful* toward God.
   (4) They became vain and proud of their mental processes and discussions.
   (5) Their hearts became darkened because of their pride of intellect.
   (6) Boasting of their own wisdom they ignored the wisdom of God and thus became fools.
   (7) They worshipped perishable images instead of the imperishable God. In reality people exchanged places with their Creator, worshipping what *they* had created, instead of the One who had created them.

Any one can slip into the non-Christian experience by this natural sequence. The point which determines the issue is described in Isaiah 50 : 10, 11. It all depends on whether we walk in our own light or in the light of God as we see it in the face of Jesus Christ. What is our source of light? Is it our own ideas or the truth of God?

II. *The steps out of the non-Christian life.*

   (1) Read Heb. 3 : 7–13, 19. "If ye shall hear his voice, harden not your hearts." Think of what we lose if we delay listening; *e. g.*, see Deut. 1 : 2–3. It took the Israelites forty years to go eleven days' journey because of their hardness of heart. See Heb. 3 : 8, 9.
   (2) *Receive* the truth. See John 1 : 12, "receiving" and "believing" are used here interchangeably. Read Matt. 18 : 3 for the teaching about the child heart. "Become" a little child implies a process of growth even if one "be" not a child.
   (3) Recognize the *sin* of *unbelief*, as in John 1 : 11, the awful sin of breaking the connection between ourselves and God—who "*made us for him-*

self." Have I a right to rob God of myself, whom He made for His own possession?

(4) Heb. 4 : 1–2. We must recognize that we come short of His best because the word of hearing was not united by *faith.* God has the *right* to speak to the heart that He has made; therefore one should receive it in childlike faith and trust.

(5) Read Heb. 4 : 6–11. We must deal with the spirit of disobedience. This centres around our will. "See that ye refuse not him that speaketh." Heb. 12 : 25. The promises of Jesus in John 7 : 17 and John 14 : 21 are then to be tested by any one who will prove their truth by obedience.

(6) Read Matt. 11 : 28 and I John 1 : 8–10. Begin to open the mind to the invitation of Jesus Christ and take Him at His word.

(7) Luke 11 : 13. Begin to exercise the privilege of a child and *ask* for the Holy Spirit. Let us humble ourselves before God and thank Him for His willingness to receive us. See Phil. 4 : 6, 7. In this way we create the right attitude of heart toward God and begin to form the habit of dependence on Him for all our need and all our life.

(8) See Romans 8 : 1–3 and Romans 8 : 16. We then come to know the freedom that comes when the spirit of life in Christ Jesus begins to work in us changing our former unworthy and selfish desires into holy and unselfish yearnings. God does not force any one of us into a life with Him, but He waits for us to give Him a chance to enter in by His Spirit and transform us from within.

> "You ask me how I gave my heart to Christ?
>   I do not know.
> There came a yearning for Him in my soul
>   So long ago.
> I found earth's flowers would fade and die;
> I longed for something that could satisfy:
> And then—and then—somehow I seemed to dare
> To lift my broken heart to Him in prayer.
>   I do not know;
>   I cannot tell you how:
>   I only know
>   He is my Saviour now!"

CHAPTER XII

THE APPROACH TO THOSE WHO HAVE INTELLECTUAL DIFFICULTIES

Ever since Jesus Christ said of Himself "I am the truth" Christianity has not been afraid of any honest question nor dismayed by any discovery of new truth. The Christian faith is a natural faith based on the truth that through Jesus Christ it is possible for man to have a personal relationship with the God who made the heavens and the earth and in whom are all the treasures of wisdom and knowledge. Rejoicing in that relationship we were meant to grow up as children in our Father's house, gaining new knowledge of Him and His relation to the world, seeing in Him the One in whom all things hold together. Through history, experience, and knowledge we were meant to understand our wonderful Father, and to love Him not only with all our heart and strength but also with all our *mind*. This ideal would have been simple were it not that the dulness of people's minds has often worked sad havoc with the simplicity of their faith. Sometimes people have been baffled in their minds because the discovery of the natural laws and methods of God's working were so slowly made that faith seemed only a mystery with no rational basis of intellectual surety. Some people with a false sense of reverence for God have thought it wrong to question the why or how of God's workings and have exacted a blind unreasoning faith from others and so done violence to that mental integrity which God gave us. Often, too, in blindness or pride of heart men have thought that they could see *all* the truth and have exalted their interpretation of it as the standard for entrance into the kingdom of God; thus many have been caused to stumble, because they could not give their mental consent. There have been others also who expected of little children the mental acquiescence of adult life, forgetting the parable of the kingdom, in which our Lord spoke of the law of growth: "First the blade, then the ear, then the full corn in the ear," and many of these children fell back in dismay and mental confusion. It often happens that the emphasis of one truth to the exclusion of others has produced a distorted gospel which has made people question and turn away puzzled by such a picture of Christianity.

These and other experiences through which the Christians of all ages have wandered in their search to know God ought to make us tender in our sympathy with those who as naturally ask "Why?" and "How?" regarding spiritual matters as our little children ask their many questions in getting acquainted with their little world. Especially in these days of the twentieth century are we full of new questions regarding God and His revelation through Jesus Christ. Science has revealed the marvellous workings of natural law bringing new assurance to our faith in God, and at the same time raising new questions. Historical research has dug out the very roots of our faith and made us reconstruct some of our theories, while it has shed new light on the sources of our confidence. The fire and the sword are turning upside down our ideas about Christian living and civilization. The ease with which all the secrets of knowledge are accessible and open to every boy and girl makes each one of them a walking question-mark if they have any mental life at all. When we add to all this the struggles of mental adolescence to which every college student is keenly alive it seems as though no service could be more important than helping our friends to-day to find their Lord towering above all the wisdom of the world and to see all of it related rationally to Him.

As we look at the perplexity of people we find that the time when questions of faith are most nerve-racking is during those years that mark the mental transition from youth to maturity. Between the ages of fifteen and twenty-five the strain is greatest. During this time we put a question-mark after nearly every statement and demand that beliefs should meet the test of reason and experience. To none does this period of mental adolescence bring more difficulties than to the sincere Christian. In the realm of the religious life the suffering is keenest. Especially is this true with those whose Christianity has been a habit of life into which they have grown naturally because of home training and example, or have inherited along with furniture and family traditions. The authority of parents and the pastor of the home church have been all-compelling—sometimes *too* compelling. Often the religious teaching has been so dogmatic and positive that the mind of the child has reacted against it and refuses to be acquiescent. The same effect may be produced by certain kinds of religious reading:

> " Books that prove
> God's being so definitely, that man's doubt
> Grows self-defined the other side the line,
> Made atheist by suggestion; moral books,
> Exasperating to license."
>
> (*Mrs. E. B. Browning.*)

Out of the protecting influences of home life that have shielded them from those persons and points of view that would counteract home influences they are suddenly transferred to college or to business. There they meet some attractive personalities who seem to get on happily without habits of devotion. Every course in college naturally stirs up speculative thoughts; business standards do not square with religious teaching; the value of each habit of life is challenged. Father and mother are far away and even if they were near they might not be able to understand, because they may not have had a similar experience. Our Christian friend feels the necessity of restating truth in terms of life and experience, and thus the old authority is questioned. In science, literature, and philosophy one is dealt with as a rational creature and the mind is encouraged to demand reasons for its convictions. Why should not religious beliefs stand the same tests? It is just at this point that a feeling of uncertainty and loneliness drops down like a fog which grows all the blacker as the days go by. It is difficult to find sympathy or constructive help in thinking through these problems.

It is not always easy to gain the confidence of these perplexed ones. Sometimes they do not like to own up to themselves that their foundations are shaking. They are indeed fortunate if some mature Christian who has been through this experience comes into their horizon with hope, cheer, and practical help. If any one of us does come into sympathetic relations with those who are puzzled in their minds, it will be merely because we have been utterly natural with them and taken their experiences for granted as normal and inevitable. Above all things, we ought never to question their right to ask questions—that is God-given—and who are we that we should take it away?

In helping people to a reasonable faith we should use chiefly the natural counsels of common sense that we can all accept, trusting that these will be the steadying power that in time will bring mental poise and satisfaction. It is quiet confidence and reassurance that we all need at such times and a sane appreciation of the laws of our mental growth. In mental stress it is well to recall the following points:

(1) *Many questions relating to religious faith need time for their answer.* The mind is likely to be impatient and demand *immediate* satisfaction in the manner of a small child who can unconsciously ask questions far beyond its ability to understand. If a person can be persuaded to face doubts honestly, noting them down and then quietly putting them aside, time will bring unexpected evidence. It is not a mark of intellectual cowardice to "call time" on questions of faith. A distinguished scholar once showed a friend a little note-book which he carried with him continually. In it he noted some queries that had occurred to him as he read or listened to others. He put them down so that at some convenient time he might read and find answers to them. He said it had often been his experience that a month or so later when he would take out his book and look at his questions many of them could be crossed off at once because they had been so fully answered by some experience or chance reading that he had done. In fact, it seemed as though everything in life combined to give him light if only he stated his question clearly and gave it time. It takes strength of mind to be quiet in mind and resist the temptation to have mental Saint Vitus's dance through that impatience of spirit which says: "I want what I want when I want it." It is a sign of youth in ourselves that we must recognize and be patient with, while at the same time we discipline ourselves in self-control.

(2) *It is well often to recall the words of Saint Paul: "Now I know in part."* However deeply one may go in the search for knowledge, there are questions to puzzle the mind and baffle the thinking. These are beyond present experience and lure us on to greater discoveries in future. There are, however, some things that we know in part, and they are sufficient to direct the course to-day and form a foundation for the thinking of

to-morrow. There is no doubt, for example, that it is the revealed will of God that we should be honest, and pure, and loving. Let us take these simple, well-known revelations of God—they are not so simple as they seem—and give them full sway in every detail of daily life. It will be strange indeed if we do not feel rebuked for ever supposing that we could be intrusted with more light when we discern so dimly these fundamental facts of God's character. The classic illustration of the spiritual experience of Horace Bushnell is a case in point. It is vividly described as follows:

"Is there, then, no truth that I do believe? Yes, there is this one, now that I think of it: there is a distinction of right and wrong that I never doubted, and I see not how I can; I am even quite sure of it." Then forthwith starts up the question: "Have I, then, ever taken the principle of right for my law? I have done right things as men speak; have I ever thrown my life out on the principle to become all it requires of me? No, I have not, consciously I have not. Ah! then, here is something for me to do! No matter what becomes of my questions—nothing ought to become of them if I cannot take a first principle, so inevitably true, and live in it." The very suggestion seems to be a kind of revelation; it is even a relief to feel the conviction it brings. "Here, then," he says, "will I begin. If there is a God, as I rather hope there is, and very dimly believe, he is a right God. If I have lost him in wrong, perhaps I shall find Him in right. Will He not meet me, or perchance, even be discovered to me?" Now the decisive moment is come. He drops on his knees, and there he prays to the dim God, dimly felt, confessing the dimness for honesty's sake, and asking for help that he may begin a right life. He bows himself on it as he prays, choosing it to be henceforth his unalterable, eternal endeavor."

"It is an awfully dark prayer, in the look of it; but the truest and best he can make, . . . and the prayer and the vow are so profoundly meant that his soul is borne up into God's help. . . . He rises, and it is as if he had gotten wings. . . . After this all troublesome doubt of God's reality is gone; for he has found Him! A being so profoundly felt must inevitably be."

(3) *We need to guard the action of the mind that the emphasis be placed on positive rather than negative thinking.* Cling to what is

known and constructive and do not let the burden of what is yet to be learned make us incapable of action now. Let us use all we do know now. We do not refuse to push an electric-light button merely because we do not understand the laws of electricity; we use the knowledge we have and in the very use of it learn more of the mysterious beyond. Almost everything in life begins with a fact and ends in a mystery. It is the glory of our humanity that we are in such a world and can grow in knowledge and discover for ourselves each day a larger world which does not contradict the smaller world of yesterday but adds to its horizon. It is fortunate for us that there are so many books available for help in finding foundations for faith. Courage will come from seeing how thoughtful men have long been aware of the mental difficulties concerning faith and how they are meeting them constructively.

(4) *Do not neglect the usual forms of Christian service and the study of the gospels, even though there may be much mental uncertainty.* Through this practical laboratory work light will come. One may not be able to give light to another who is mentally befogged, but inspiring them to do practical service for those in physical, social, or moral need will be a wholesome tonic for their faith. A distinguished theological professor who went through years of mental questioning says that his faith in God's power was constantly reaffirmed by his experience three nights a week in a rescue mission where he had to help sin-stained men into a new life. The effort to win them drove him back to the promises of Christ.

One often finds students who suspend all the activities of the Christian life and their habits of worship through a mistaken sense of honesty. They accuse themselves of hypocrisy and say: "How can I worship at church and engage in prayer when I'm not sure what I believe? At least I will be honest and not pretend to be something that I am not." And with a sense of heroic virtue they withdraw from all the atmosphere that would stimulate and inspire them in their search for sincerity and cut themselves off from some of the sources of spiritual help. They would not think of applying such logic to college experiences in science or mathematics. Suppose they failed to grasp some scientific principle. Would it be an evidence of honesty to say: "I do not understand that principle. I will not work any longer in the laboratory or study the text-book, for it would be hypocritical"? No, any sincere student would consider it necessary to double the time spent in study and to seek to know the mysterious scientific principle by ever more thorough and painstaking laboratory work. By the same method spiritual fog is dispelled.

(5) *It is reasonable to expect that light on the Christian life will come most quickly through a closer study of the sources contained in the New Testament.* No opinion of men *about* Jesus Christ can compare in value with going directly to his teachings and meeting the challenge of his words and personality. It is a test of our sincerity—Doctor Coe emphasizes this in writing on this subject. "The intellectual tactics most likely to be helpful in such cases consist less in the direct refutation of the doubt than in the wider opening out of the problem through which the doubt arises. A larger horizon is often sufficient. A doubt as to the inspiration of the Scriptures can best be met by exhibiting the growth of the self-revelation of God of which the Scriptures are a record. . . . Similarly, doubts as to the person of Christ may well be met by intensive study of His life as a whole and a broad study of the place that He occupies in the general religious history of humanity."

(6) *In searching for light on intellectual questions one needs to examine the inner motives for this search and ask often: "Why do I want to know these things?* Do I want light because of my interest in the workings of the brain and the mental stimulus of added knowledge, or am I searching for light in order to find out the will of God and *do* it?" Knowledge of spiritual truth involves the relationship between two living spirits, God the infinite Spirit, and the human, finite spirit. In order to know the truth there must be an honest will to obey and follow the light as it is revealed by the Father of light, with whom every human life must inevitably reckon. The Christian must at least have the mental attitude of the pagan in whose lips Richard Watson Gilder puts the words:

> "If Jesus Christ is a man,—
> And only a man,—I say
> That of all mankind I cleave to him
> And to him will I cleave alway.

> "If Jesus Christ is a God,—
> And the only God,—I swear
> I will follow Him through heaven and hell,
> The earth, the sea, the air." (*R. W. Gilder.*)

(7) *A right attitude of spirit is as essential as a right attitude of will.* The humble receptive heart of a little child is sure to grow in knowledge. Jesus made this a condition of entering the kingdom of heaven, and adds that "Whoso shall humble himself as this little child the same is greatest in the kingdom of heaven." The besetting sin of the mind is likely to be intellectual pride and presumption. It often insists on paring down a subject to the dimensions of its own limited capacity. Some one has defined scepticism as the friction that results when a small mind tries to take in all at once a very big idea. Our mental confusion ought to be a reflection on our own finiteness rather than an occasion for challenging the teaching of Christ.

There is need to recall often the character of God and rest in the faith that He is working with a love and wisdom that takes into account all seeming contradictions between the world as it is and as it ought to be. And this is reinforced by the promise of Jesus that the Spirit of God "shall guide you into all the truth" and "take of mine and shall declare it unto you" (John 16 : 13, 14).

(8) *The yearning for light and the persistent prayer for help will always find an answer.* This may come in a number of ways. There will be a growing spirit of discernment and an awareness of what is true so that the mind will be able to sift evidence and judge facts more fairly. Then, too, day by day, experience will be added which will confirm many things that seemed dogmatic and unreal before. "The path of the righteous is as the dawning light that shineth more and more unto perfect day" (Prov. 4 : 18). Daily living with others will disclose sources of strength or weakness that will vitalize some truth that seemed hitherto unimportant. And light will also come through added knowledge. This help will come through the books written by honest thinkers who dare to face issues and think their way out to clear conclusions. All this available knowledge is part of God's reply to the sincere thinker. There are some things that have been proven and the student may well build upon the knowledge of others.

(9) *An open-minded student cannot get very far afield if the authority of Christ is recognized in all matters pertaining to God.* Every one bows to some authority, though he may not be willing to own to it, and instinctively follows some one who seems

to be an echo of his thinking. Many students are dazzled by some personality who seems to move along brilliantly unhampered by tradition. They trail along in the wake of his meteoric dust, not realizing that they are not really independent thinkers. Sooner or later they wake up to the limitations of the one they follow. Now, if we are bound to follow some personality why not accept the authority of Jesus Christ as a working hypothesis? Even though at first the mind may not understand the mystery of his personality and may challenge His claims, yet we are driven back constantly to His life and teaching as the final revelation of God. Whatever else man may see in Jesus Christ, the world recognizes at least that He is the great specialist in the knowledge of God and in the realm of character. And because He is the great specialist we do well to bow to His authority. One does not compromise his intellectual life by taking the teachings of Christ as a working hypothesis to be tested in the laboratory of life. All progress in science is made by this method. We obey the directions of the specialist and work them out by experiment. Then the mind is convinced and the knowledge is truly ours. We use wireless telegraphy even before we understand it; we take most of our daily life on faith. Can we do any less with the teachings of Jesus Christ? To recognize and yield to His right to be followed implicitly is to open the door into a large free country where peace, order, and satisfaction abide. We make the final test of truth by proving its power in life, and then a compelling conviction will come, that Jesus Christ is as He claimed, "the way, the truth, and the life."

BIBLE STUDY XII

KNOWING AND BELIEVING

I. *The open door to spiritual verity.*

Read John 3 : 1–21. Nicodemus, a type of the earnest intellectual man who is deeply interested in all religious questions. His mental curiosity was more concerned with the method and process by which Jesus worked miracles than with the fact of the sign as bringing God near. The key to his attitude is revealed by the words *"How can"* in verses 4 and 9. He takes for granted that the measure of his mind must be the measure of his religion. In answering him Jesus opens the door into the great regions beyond the facts of human experience and states the laws by which alone we can understand the things of God. Nicodemus was neglecting to use

INTELLECTUAL DIFFICULTIES 103

the eye of his heart because he was so sure that the eyes of his mind were his surest guides. In common with many modern students he needed to realize the truth that Mrs. Browning discerned:

> "All this anguish in the thick
> Of men's opinions . . . press and counterpress,
> Now up, now down, now underfoot, and now
> Emergent . . . all the best of it, perhaps,
> But throws you back upon a noble trust
> And use of your own instinct,—merely proves
> Pure reason stronger than bare inference
> At strongest. Try it,—fix against heaven's wall
> Your scaling ladders of high logic—mount
> Step by step!—Sight goes faster; that still ray
> Which strikes out from you, how, you cannot tell,
> And why, you know not—(did you eliminate,
> That such as you, indeed, should analyze?)
> Goes straight and fast as light, and high as God."

II. *The miracle of the illumined heart.*

(1) Read again verses 3, 5, and 6. Compare them with John 23, 24. On what does every true personal relationship depend? Study I Cor. 1 : 20, 21 and 2 : 11, 14, and write down in your own words the way Paul explains the teaching of Jesus. How do we enter into the experience of being "born again"? See Luke 11 : 13. What is the connection between being "born of the spirit" and intellectual growth? See John 16 : 12–14.

(2) Read John 1 : 4. Is there such a thing as truth in the realm of spirit apart from life and personality? in the case of love, purity, honesty, etc.? Life becomes a laboratory for light and intellectual perception. Read again John 3 : 16, 19, 20, 21. What is the cause of moral blindness in verse 20? What is the challenge that Jesus makes to every one who finds it difficult to believe in Him? See verses 18, 19. What has to be settled before one can expect to see the truth? See Matt. 5 : 8 and John 12 : 46. Jesus said: "I am the truth," "I am the light of the world." If we say we want to know truth and yet do not come to Him who is truth what is the inference?

(3) Light comes only to the receptive, open mind and to the heart of a little child. See Matt. 18 : 3. Note the force of the word *"become"* which implies a process. A person may not *be* a little child and yet *become* one. See I Cor. 13 : 12 for two expressions of Paul's childlike mind which knows it does not see fully and makes many mistakes in judgment. What is the comfort of the child relationship with our Lord? See John 10 : 26–29.

> "I lost breath in my soul sometimes,
> And cried, 'God save me if there's any God,'
> But, even so, God saved me; and being dashed
> From error on to error, every turn
> Still brought me nearer to the central truth."
> (*Mrs. Browning, Aurora Leigh.*)

(4) The life in Christ is imparted by exposing the heart to the infection of His teachings. See John 5 : 39, 40, John 7 : 37, and John 8 : 12, also

John 6 : 63. All spiritual truth taught by others is only the diluted teaching of Jesus Christ. Why are we so reluctant to get into close quarters with His teaching?

(5) Obedience to the word of Christ is the condition for knowing the truth. See John 7 : 17. "He that willeth to *do* . . . shall *know*." What does Jesus promise we shall know? What other rewards are promised to those who obey? See John 14 : 21.

(6) The gift of the Spirit—the indwelling God—is the great gift that alone helps us to know the truth. Luke 11 : 13 and I Cor. 2 : 12. Can we be honest and sincere and meet these conditions? We can never say again truthfully that we are wanting to know the truth if we do not face this challenge of Jesus Christ. We do not need more of God, but God needs more of us—needs to possess more of our attention and thoughts— "bringing every thought into captivity to the obedience of Christ" (II Cor. 10 : 5).

CHAPTER XIII

THE APPROACH TO THOSE WHO ARE FIGHTING BESETTING SINS

"Character," Booker T. Washington once said, "is the sum of all we struggle against." It is the pure metal that abides the fire and the pressure and the long process of testing. There is something in us that will not let us rest in the fight because God has put into us spirits that tend to be like Him. We cannot be satisfied unless we are victors. When our spirits have once looked into the face of God we become aware of two facts—we see what we must be if we are to be fit to live with Him, and we see ourselves as we are, stained by our choice of sin, weaker than wee babes, discouraged by the seeming hopelessness of ever freeing our spirits from the chains of the flesh. There are many people who have just seen enough of God to be conscious of their losing fight, and yet have not seen enough to know that the heart of the gospel lies in bringing power to us all to win out through our Lord Jesus Christ. The fact of life to which each of us bears witness is that we are bound for a destiny—which is conditioned by character; that character we must have, and it is to be won only by a struggle against great odds, but possible through a strength not our own imparted by God through Jesus Christ. What then is more worth while than to help people to find this strength of God? We can really help others in no permanent way if we cannot help them here. Now, in order to help others, we ourselves need to understand the situation and face the fact that struggle was meant to give us wings and not weights. Otherwise we may be like many who resent having to fight and with a cynical spirit look upon themselves as victims of the scheme of things, so losing their conception of a loving heavenly Father. The popularity of writings like the *Rubaiyat* of Omar Khayam and that of kindred pagans bears witness to a sympathy with his cynicism which many a modern student of life shares.

And yet Omar Khayam recognized the first fundamental fact in the situation when he said:

> "I sent my soul out in the Invisible
> Some letter of the After Life to spell:
> And by and by my soul returned and answered:
> 'I, myself, am heaven and hell.' "

In other words each of us is here with a capacity for being either heaven or hell; we have an equal chance to be one thing or the other. The capacity is within us; it is not alone due to the scheme of things.

We are also responsible moral agents. Sin is not ignorance gone astray; we have the power to choose according to our desire. The choices of many of us may be few, but there is always some one choice between good and evil to be made, and we are responsible only for the scope of choices that each of us has. We see these choices worked out so often in the same family. Two children with the same parents, the same environment, the same chances for choice will develop utterly different characters; one may have always desired to make right choices and the other may have desired to make wrong choices. The capacity for desire was the same, the choice different—the character in the end just what each had made it.

The third fact is that strength grows by exercise with obstacles; it is the fight that gives interest to life. The football team only grows strong by facing an opposing team: the game is interesting only if it is a close one. The doctor longs for a difficult case in order that his skill may be tested. A girl plays a brilliant sonata only through the exercise of many hours of practising. We train our wills to do the will of God only by repeated choices of the right in the face of alluring by-paths.

The fourth fact that we need to face is that we are so made that often our will gets more strength on the rebound than by direct pressure. "I never was really truthful," said a friend, "until I had to work by the side of a woman who was habitually insincere and circuitous. It filled me with such loathing that I determined to be sincere always." The will often gains self-control by having to face unrestrained impatience in others. In fact, we seem to learn from concrete object-lessons in what is wrong to turn from it to God. The presence of darkness makes us appreciate the light.

It is also this consciousness of imperfection that may open up the beauties of a filial relation with God. Our mothers are dear to us because of the patience with which they guided us through our days of weakness and uncontrol until we caught their spirit and ideals and reverenced their love which stood the test of all our failures and faults. So in a more wonderful way we grow to know the love of God through our crying out in the dark and hearing His voice, through our need of forgiveness and counsel, through the pull of the ideal as we see it in Him, through the gift of his strength, and through the yielding up of our desires to His will in an obedience that brings rest.

Finally, it helps us to face the struggle when we realize that all the strong and lasting things in life cost pain and a long fight. We must be worth an infinite price, each of us, because it takes so long to weld our characters. "How soon can you educate my boy?" asked a man of a school principal; "I don't want him to go through a lot of unnecessary grind." "That depends on what you want to make of him," came the reply. "God can make a squash in three months, but it takes one hundred years to make an oak." It is our destiny that makes the long fight against wind and storm and cold both necessary and worth while, and the sooner we gird us up for the fray to fight to a finish the sooner the victory will come. "This is how I run," says Paul, "not being in any doubt as to my goal."

The fight with besetting sins, those that keep us from obeying our Lord, generally centres around some root or central sin, the especial weak spot in each of us. It may be the enthralling slavery of some gross sin of the flesh, or selfishness may be the pivotal centre of our hearts, or we may be mesmerized by the lure of the world. From these three roots come the many branches of wrong choices that overgrow our hearts, shut out the light, and make us spiritual anæmics. It does no good to lop off the branches so long as we fail to deal with the taproot. Much of the discouragement about ourselves, which we often try to shake off by plausible excuses, comes because we fail to deal with the root of all our besetting sins.

In facing the fight we need to go about it with a skill born of the experience that those who have won out have gained. There is help for all of us who are willing to be taught. Our experience is not unique but the common lot of the race and there are rules of the game that we need to heed.

(1) *We need to define our own particular sin in its root-form and own up to it to ourselves and to God.* It is not hard to find out. Let us look at the things that are the line of least resistance in us. The joy in a vulgar joke, the itching for gossip and scandal, the desire to seem sophisticated and accustomed to things that soil ideals and smirch our purity, the amused smile over the innocent spirit, the delight in impure books and mental pictures may reveal to us a spirit that loves impurity and a heart that is sensual at the core. We shrink from owning up to anything so hideous, but we shall not get far until we shock ourselves by seeing our sin just as it is.

It may be another trail, however, that leads to the home of our poverty-stricken spirit. Perhaps our weak point may be discovered to us by a habit of self-pity and the imagining of unreal situations in which we are always the star actors; by reluctance to give others their due of praise or opportunity, by content with our own righteousness, by jealousy of our friends and their happiness or success, by chafing over neglect and lack of appreciation; by a misuse of our personal power over others; by a conviction that people are wilfully refusing to see how wonderful we are and by our resentment of criticism. Under all these "natural" weaknesses lies the ugly fact that we are self-centred and selfish. It isn't easy to accept this inflated ego as an exact picture of ourselves, but we must look at it until we loathe it, or there is no deliverance for us.

But perhaps our portrait has other features. It may be outlined by the fear of what "they" may say or think, the love of excitement, the panting to keep up with the chase, the living beyond one's strength and means, the dread of being alone, the fear of being unlike others, the desire for self-indulgence and luxury, and the subtle influence of false standards. We can excuse ourselves for being drawn into these weaknesses, but we are silent when we see that in reality we are living a lie and losing our souls because we love the world more than we love our life and our God. Soon people will see our shrivelled spirits and laugh at our folly. There is no peace for us until we see ourselves as we really are at heart—insincerity posing as sincerity.

(2) *Having defined and owned to our sin, we need to recall that it is not God's will that we should be slaves of sin.* There is no need that I should be a captive one moment longer than I really

want to be. I can face my own weakness and say with truth, "It is impossible for me to break this slavery in my own strength," but in the same breath I can also say, "The things that are impossible with men are possible with God"; "If any man thirst let him come unto me and drink, and from within him shall flow rivers of living water"; "By grace are ye saved through faith, and that *not of yourselves ;* it is the gift of God." The whole message of the gospel of Jesus Christ is meaningless if it does not work in my case. It *must* if I meet the needful tests. If I cannot believe in God, I cannot believe in anything. But I must believe in His power; because it has worked in other lives, therefore it can work in mine.

(3) *Let us deal with our sin at its source and fight our battle in the realm of the imagination.* Every spiritual battle is lost or won in the life of our thoughts. It is what the word means which reads: "Keep thy heart with all diligence; for out of it are all the issues of life." The temptation usually comes in when we relax our minds and let the door stand open; when we "let ourselves go" a prey to any wandering thoughts. It is the ungirded mind that is open to swift attack. The temptation also comes upon the heels of self-pity; when we begin to be sorry for ourselves and let self instead of our Lord get the reins into its hands. The minute we are in control of self we are in the control of weakness. There is no wolf in sheep's clothing quite so demoralizing to our strength as self-pity in the realm of our imagination. Much of our besetting sin would never get in to us if we were prepared by having in our minds a number of subjects for thought that are truthful and lawful, interesting and creative. It is here that we need also to incarnate the living Christ so that we shall *never* be alone in our minds but find every thought hallowed by His presence, open to His scrutiny. In God's presence our heart and thought must face the desires of the flesh, our self-love and our insincere bondage to the world; we can then get from Him a clean heart and holy desires, giving up fully our very selves to be dealt with by Him.

The next step for victory forms a working programme for the daily life of any one who sincerely wants God to rule in his life. It is merely the practical application of modern psychology to the situation by which any one may take advantage of natural reinforcements that are available in the daily fight with sin. It is well to recall a few of these helps.

(1) *Crowd out the tempting thought by diverting the attention to some other interesting subject.* We cannot subdue our emotions but we can will to think hard of something else until the wrong emotions die a natural death. It follows also that the more interests we have that absorb and fascinate, the easier it is to turn from the one that brings a temptation to others that hold us. It is a good thing to develop as many points of contact with life as possible. Often a temptation loses its power to cast a spell over us because of a wider horizon and a larger life which bring a new scale of values. It is well to have at hand some clever books that hold the attention or some enjoyable task that needs our concentrated effort or some friends to whom we can turn whenever we find ourselves swept along by sudden temptations. When we know our danger-points it is the part of common sense to guard against them in advance by some such definite preparation.

(2) *Remember that the mind is held by the positive thought on which it is concentrated.* Many of us have had the baffling experience of praying intensely to be delivered from the grip of a certain sin and then rising from our knees to go forth and commit that sin before an hour has passed. It seems as if prayer did not help. The reason for our failure is hid in the fact that it was the wrong kind of prayer that failed to meet conditions and brought no help. A friend said that years ago, when she was trying to ride a bicycle, she never failed to run into a telegraph-pole if she looked at it; that she found that her eye instinctively guided her hand. The law is the same in prayer. When we focus our thought in prayer intensely on our sin we are consciously holding our attention on that sin, and the mind thus held by the positive thought is controlled by it in its acts. The reason why prayer is such a resource for a tempted spirit is that in the presence of God we have the most powerful stimulus to *forget* our sin and to remember and adore Him in all His power and beauty and holiness. Sin cannot abide in His sight, and if we come to Him recalling our relation to Him as little children and letting Him absorb our attention and thrill our hearts with the sense of His friendship, we rise up so bathed in the thought of Him that an evil thought has no welcome in our hearts. Thus deliverance comes. It

is a help to commit to memory certain of the psalms of praise and filial trust like the 23d and 121st and the 90th; also portions of the gospels, like the 10th chapter of John, for the express purpose of using them in prayer to recall God to our minds.

In the same way we can change a wrong spirit that is in us. For example, we cannot pray for some one who has injured us until our unforgiving spirit is changed by the thought of our Lord. We need to remember His wonderful love when He prayed, "Father, forgive them," and the patience that He has with us in all our stumblings, although we fail Him so pitifully. Then, when the thought of the one who has sinned against us is lost in the thought of our relation to Him, we find that we are able to pray honestly for our stumbling friends and the victory of a forgiving spirit comes.

(3) *We turn most easily to thoughts that have become habitual.* The secret of lasting moral victory depends, humanly speaking, upon the reinforcement of holy desires, memories, and habits of thought that have been stored up within us during the years. The practice of daily Bible reading and meditation is one of the means of opening our minds to the influence of Christ and giving Him a chance to control our thinking. If we keep ourselves steadily in the atmosphere of such pure and true fellowship we will find that memories of these experiences will come back to help and steady us in time of need. It is the work of God's Spirit, Jesus says, to "bring to your remembrance all that I said unto you." Therefore the habit of thinking daily about the teaching of Christ takes on new value in view of the help it will bring to us later in the fire of temptation. The experience of countless Christians bears witness to the truth of this promise. It helps us also to know that Jesus met His temptations through His memory of the Scripture, thus confirming the word of the Psalmist: "Thy word have I hid in my heart that I might not sin against Thee" (Psalm 119 : 11).

(4) *Begin to help some one else to overcome temptation.* There is nothing that helps more in our own struggle for character than to feel responsible for putting strength into another who trusts us. If we are sincere, it will lead us to moral victory. In fact, our sincerity is a big stimulus to our wills. We cannot give any one else what we have not ourselves, and if we urge others to win we too *must* win to keep our moral integrity. The sense of companionship in a moral struggle also brings

help. Our friends take courage when they know that we, too, are making the same fight. It does not seem so hopeless and impossible to them when we tell them they can win a victory through Jesus Christ if they see that we understand the strength of the enemy and have found help in reply to prayer. It is one of the glorious privileges of our imperfect, stumbling life to find help for ourselves and for others too even before we have attained. As Forbes Robinson writes: "To help a brother up the mountain while you yourself are only just able to keep your foothold, to struggle through the mist together—that surely is better than to stand at the summit and beckon" (*Forbes Robinson's Letters to His Friends*, p. 118).

(5) *We need also to build up a margin of physical health as an aid to self-control.* We have already seen, in Chapter VII, the relation of surplus nervous energy to the power of self-control. When we are facing the question of moral victory everything relating to our daily living becomes important as an aid or hindrance to our spiritual vigor. We cannot be honest before God and ignore the means of storing up nervous energy. "Whether therefore ye eat, or drink," counsels Paul, "or whatsoever ye do, do all to the glory of God." Food and exercise, sleep and interests that are varied and wholesome become sacred responsibilities. Especially too must we guard against the weakness of overfatigue lest an unfair advantage be taken by the desires of our flesh. It is during times of fatigue that the fight is hardest.

(6) *The friendship of Christ and the trust He puts in us will be a spur to victory.* The trust of others calls forth all our sense of honor and loyalty. We do not want to fail our friends who expect us to be strong. In the same way, the life of friendship with our Lord holds us to our best if only we will keep ourselves under the spell of it. "He that abideth in me and I in him, the same bringeth forth much fruit," Jesus says to his disciples, and the inference is that we cannot help bringing forth fruit if we meet the test of the "abiding" life. If we *do* abide, then temptation is an opportunity to prove to our Lord that we are trustworthy; that we do not fail Him in the crisis. Finally, we learn that no temptation is so strong that it may not be overcome. The promise is indeed true that a way of escape is open to us if we will take it. Even in our severest temptations there is a time when we debate with ourselves whether

or not we will yield, and then if we do yield it is because we have deliberately decided to do so in the face of our conscience or in spite of the remembrance of God. We *could* have chosen to listen to Him if we had wanted to listen. The fact that we are so ashamed to go to God at once to begin again forgiven and cleansed is in itself a witness to the truth that we could have overcome. Even if this has been our experience let us never fall deeper into sin by staying away from Him in our shame. Let us begin anew in His strength, humbled yet determined to win at all costs. It all goes back to the will, to the honesty with which we can yield our wills to God with a pledge of obedience that grows easier as we see how He works in quiet patience to make us "all glorious within."

BIBLE STUDY XIII
Fighting Sin

I. *The conflict within.*

Read Romans 7 : 19–8 : 1, 2. "The good which I would I do not: but the evil which I would not, that I practise." This is the cry of every honest spirit. The battle is hopeless without the transcendent power of the Holy Spirit bringing us into freedom to do the right because the principle of obedience to the will of Jesus Christ is permanently settled. In the conflict of inner desires, one must be *willing* that the Holy Spirit *shall win out* even though it means a fight. Have I definitely decided the issues between Christ and self in my life? Can I honestly say that the Spirit of God is gaining fuller control day by day?

> "This should have been a noble creature: he
> Hath all the energy which would have made
> A goodly frame of glorious elements,
> Had they been wisely mingled: as it is,
> It is an awful chaos—light and darkness,
> And mind and dust, and passions and pure thoughts,
> Mixed, and contending without end or order—
> All dormant or destructive: he will perish
> And yet he must not."
>
> *(Byron.)*

II. *What sin means.*

See I John 3 : 4–5—"lawlessness." Everything in the world is obedient to law and controlled by God. Man alone has the power and desire to become lawless and thus break the harmony of the universe.

See I John 1 : 5–10. We cannot live in fellowship with God if we walk in darkness; so sin breaks our relationship with the One on whom we must depend for everything we are and have. Read also Psalm 66 : 18 and Isaiah 59 : 1–2.

Read Romans 6 : 23. The end of sin is death—the wasting of all our powers. Can we afford to face such possibilities? Why is it that we or others go on without settling the question?

III. *Some motives that help us in our fight.*

Romans 8 : 15 and I John 3 : 1–3. The consciousness that we are God's children and we must be worthy of Him.

Eph. 4 : 30. The Spirit of God yearns over us with such patience and watchfulness and is so faithful in speaking to our conscience that this remembrance ought to keep us from grieving Him.

Heb. 12 : 1. The witnesses to the power of God all about us and the friends who trust us ought to call out every bit of determination in us to win out for their sakes.

Acts 4 : 12. If we do not win the victory through Jesus Christ, all is lost. There is no other hope for us. All is at stake.

Questions

Which motive makes the strongest appeal and why? How can we develop an increasing sensitiveness to the approach of temptation?

IV. *How God reinforces us in temptation.*

John 14 : 26. Some holy memory is brought to our mind. If God uses our memory to help us, what is our responsibility in storing up material that he can use?

Ezek. 36 : 25–27, 31. The miracle of the clean heart and new desires makes the impossible possible. In what two ways are the old desires overcome? See verses 27 and 31. What are the conditions that we must meet in order to have the gift of the new heart?

I Cor. 10 : 13. God provides the way of escape. No temptation is so strong that it cannot be conquered in God's strength. It is the experience of us all that in every temptation there is a calm moment when we decide whether or not we will yield. We decide the issue in our minds first before it gets into our action. We can escape if we will to do so. God does remind us in the still small voice; the responsibility is ours if we do not listen. What way of victory does Paul show in Romans 8 : 1–17? Describe his conception of our relation to Christ by which we may be made free from the law of sin and death.

V. *The safeguard against temptation.*

James 1 : 12–18 and Phil. 4 : 8, 9. Temptation comes when we are led away by our own desires. Through the appeal of whatever is beautiful, true, and honest, we can fill our minds with thoughts of these things, and throw all our energy into working for them until our minds are too fully occupied to give room to selfish desire. If we enter on some service for others that will commit us to the higher interests of life we will find ourselves held true even by the dependence and trust of others in us, and we will not dare fail them. Let us do everything in our power to let self-sacrificing love grow in our hearts that it may hold us in our time of need.

CHAPTER XIV

THE APPROACH TO THOSE WHO FACE PROBLEMS OF CONDUCT

The decision to give one's life to God through obedience to Jesus Christ as Saviour and Master and Friend is a definite act of the will that may take place in a moment of time; but the working out of the Christlike character in conduct is a process of a lifetime. The inner states and desires of the heart control not only the conscious thoughts of our minds but also the conduct of life in the outer world. That which is in the heart inevitably reveals itself in word, in deed, and in physical effects such as the very expression of our faces and tones of our voices. Character is formed by the repeated actions of our will, which carries out the inner desires of the heart. People judge of our character by the habitual desires of our hearts as they express themselves in conduct. When they know these uniform desires they know what to expect in our conduct. Sometimes a desire unlike our habitual desires gains temporary mastery and expresses itself in conduct. Such conduct is a shock to our friends for two reasons: first, because it is inconsistent with what they think our character to be; and second, because it compels them to revise their judgment of us. Therefore, because "as a man thinketh in his heart, so is he," it is immensely vital to our sincerity and transparency of heart that our conduct should always square with our habitual desires. If we fail here we fail really to be Christians because of several reasons.

If our conduct is inconsistent with our desires, we are not genuine. Our outer life becomes a pose, an assumed rôle, an impersonal thing, a lie.

Because we strike a blow at our moral integrity and are in spiritual anarchy where neither our own spirit or the Spirit of God is in control.

Because when our outer conduct varies from that precise requirement of our inner desires we kill those inner desires and our character is undermined and goes to pieces. One reason why a lie is so Satanic is because in conduct it defies the reign of the most sacred part of our inner life—our moral judgment, which lies back of our consciences. When this is outraged, we face moral disaster.

Therefore, we imperil the very unity of our personalities when our friends see our conduct merely as a series of unrelated acts instead of the outshining of a steady spirit that does not swerve from its dominant desire.

<u>The secret of conduct that moulds character consists in letting our moral judgments rule the desires of our heart.</u> Our moral judgments must issue from the teaching of the Spirit of God as He reveals Himself to the humble, open, listening heart. A Christian who is giving over the daily control of his inner decisions to God in trustful obedience finds his will acting in the outer world of conduct in perfect harmony with his moral judgments. If it rebels momentarily it is quickly humbled by confession and made to make things right in obedience again. It is as Matheson says:

> "My will is not my own
> Till Thou hast made it Thine;
> If it would reach a monarch's throne,
> It must its crown resign.
> It only stands unbent
> Amid the clashing strife,
> When on Thy bosom it has leant,
> And found in Thee its life."

The difficulties of many Christians in facing the problems of conduct would be few, if only they settled the question of what should rule in their hearts, whether or not Jesus Christ should in all things occupy the foremost place; they could then quietly trust that control to express itself in conduct. The counsel we need, then, is this: it is all-important that, in dealing with conduct, we deal with our inner states and not with our outer expressions. If I get angry, no one has to tell me to flash my eyes —they obey the desire instantly; if I really love any one, no one has to tell me to be thoughtful and tender. In other words, conduct should be automatic with the inner desires.

If the natural outflow of our inner judgments and desires is to be through conduct, then we may well ask how we are guided in forming our judgments. For a Christian the path is plain: We form our moral judgments through the teachings of the Bible, especially those of Jesus Christ; through the experience of his disciples in all ages; and the impulses of the heart guided in reply to prayer. The teachings of the Bible become the norm whereby we discover the principles that accord with the Spirit of God; and as we, in prayer, submit our conduct to the daily scrutiny of our Lord, He speaks through our conscience, confirming those moral judgments that have been formed within us as a result of knowing the teaching. Therefore, it is needful that there should be constant study of the Bible if one is to be guided in the problems of conduct.

When once a moral judgment is formed, the problem of conduct respecting it ought to vanish for the Christian. For example, my moral judgment sides with God in saying that it is wrong to lie, to steal, to be impure, to hate my brother; therefore lying, stealing, impure conversation and hatred are impossible for me if my spirit rules. There is no problem of conduct in all this—there is only the problem of keeping my spirit obedient to God.

The real problems of conduct, however, centre around those things about which our moral judgments are not yet formed. It is not the problem of choosing between right and wrong, but the wisdom of choosing from among all *possible* things the best things. As the number of choices in our power grows larger the good often is the enemy of the best, and the Christian must find some active working principles that will guide in this choice so that conduct will always express our truest life.

In thinking about such principles we might list them under three heads: (1) The principles that relate to purely personal decisions affecting conduct. (2) The principles of conduct that govern our relation to others. (3) The principles of conduct that underlie our working together with God.

I. The principles that relate to purely personal decisions affecting conduct.

(1) *The intimate connection between what is a personal good and the spirit of thanksgiving to God.* We always find a quick instinctive response of gratitude when we receive something that we look upon as a good. It is one of the delicate tests that

come to mean more as we grow in Christian experience. One is not thankful for anything that is recognized instinctively as an evil. The closer we walk with God the more eagerly we long for a daily experience of the word: "The blessing of the Lord it maketh rich and addeth no sorrow therewith." Therefore, when debating whether a certain line of conduct is one that may be entered into rightly, one may well ask the question: "Can I honestly thank God for the opportunity to do this because it will bring good to my character?" If there is not a spontaneous spirit of thanksgiving arising from the conviction that this opportunity would be good for the soul, that line of conduct should be tested further by some of the following principles before committing oneself to it. This connection between what is a good and the spirit of thanksgiving is suggested in the words of Paul to Timothy. "Every creature of God is good, and nothing is to be rejected, if it be received with thanksgiving; for it is sanctified through the word of God and prayer" (I Tim. 4 : 45).

(2) *The principle of the abiding peace of God in which the conscience is at rest.* Nothing has such a hair-trigger sensitiveness in our hearts as the sense of God's peace. Any act or line of conduct that causes us to lose that sense of peace is manifestly not consistent with the inner states of the heart controlled by God's Spirit. It is a legitimate question to ask: "Is there a sense of peace in thinking of this line of conduct?" When it is withheld the chances are that one has not looked at the question from all sides or else the moral judgment has either not been placed under the clear light of God's Spirit or is warped by wilfulness. One should wait with the open, teachable heart of a little child until the sense of peace comes.

(3) *The principle of conditioned freedom.* The Christian life is a free life and not intended to be under any yoke of bondage. Its conduct is not meant to be governed by rules and regulations about *things*: We are free spirits. The guiding principles of choice in all details of conduct of a free life should centre about the question whether a given conduct, although lawful, is expedient for a certain time or place. For example, I may be free to improve my talent for music by practising two hours on a piano; but if that right conduct keeps a tired mother awake who is suffering with headache, the right thing becomes inexpedient for me because it cuts across the law of love; therefore I willingly condition my freedom for the sake of an-

other. Furthermore, we need to ask also: "Will this course of action bring me under its power and dominate me?" For example, I may enjoy the fascinations of a novel and find it often a rest and stimulus. But there may be times when it exerts such a spell over my imagination as to unfit me for days to do my duty and keep my feet on the earth. Therefore, I condition my freedom to read at all times, for the sake of a higher law that I want to obey. Yet again one should ask oneself: "Will this line of conduct give me a larger appreciation of God and strengthen His hold on my life?" This is often illustrated in the choice of our pleasures. Certain of them may leave us refreshed, exhilarated, with a sense of peace and of the beauty of God; with a new appreciation of physical relaxation and mental refreshment, that makes us open-doored to God, in new responsiveness and enthusiasm. Others may leave us without refreshment, with dulness of spirit, and a slump in our ideals. It is right to have pleasure, but if I have any care for my body as the temple of God I condition my freedom to do certain legitimate things because they do not help me to keep the spontaneous child spirit of delight in the God of all life.

II. The principles that govern our relation to others.

(1) *The principle of love applied in our own relationships will guide much of our conduct.* Love will consider another and strive to build up the life of Christ in another. The very fact that there is love in the heart implies that there is a relationship, which brings also a *responsibility* and exerts a *power* that makes it impossible for one to act independently of this relation of love. We can no longer live unto ourselves if we look at others as those to whom we owe love. The relation of love will not mean that we will always do what others want us to do. Our love must be a blend of firmness and willingness; it may mean the use of all our influence to get others to desist from some line of conduct or it may mean the giving up of our freedom to do certain things for their sakes. But the fact that we love will lead us into wise paths, although they may be different ones from what we desired.

(2) *We can often know what is right for us if we think of the principle of the social conscience which recognizes that the liberty of one must not be a stumbling-block to another.* The very fact that we do not live on a desert island but in a community of

people with whom we are socially related, involves shaping our conduct according to what is for the good of our neighbor. "Let no man seek his own, but each his neighbor's good" (I Cor. 10 : 24). It is not always easy to know where personal rights and social responsibility begin, but most of us are overzealous about our individual rights and are slow in yielding to the common good. It is the undisciplined spirit of adolescence. Freedom to think has its dangers as well as its virtues, and we want to be very sure that we are not imposing our personal point of view and preferences upon the community with which we are related. "It always used to rub me the wrong way," a girl once said, "when my mother used to say, 'Do just as you think best, my dear,' and yet I knew that if I really *did* do what I preferred the family would feel injured. Why was the issue put up to me as a personal one, when really it was a social one? Young as I was, I could see through that fallacy." We are not all as discerning as this girl or else we would not spend so much time chafing over situations in which the social conscience challenged our personal preferences. We need, rather, to learn to detect more quickly the times when this principle should take precedence and adjust our moral judgments to the social needs.

(3) *The principle of social influence also must be regarded.* There are certain lives weaker than our own in strength of character, to whom we owe a special responsibility. Our strength must not be at the expense of the weaker. It was said of our Lord: "A bruised reed he shall not break and the smoking flax he will not quench." In other words, He lived so that the bruised lives were not weakened but strengthened by His presence. This responsibility for the "little ones" of the kingdom is a big one. We are not held to account for all the weak ones of earth but for those with whom we are personally related. There are few lines of conduct so important as to lead us to shatter holy ideals or blur the moral vision of others in following them. Sometimes we need to think straight on the subject of vital moral ideals as over against personal leanings. We do not need to cease from disregarding certain ideals that some people hold if they are personal idiosyncrasies on their part and not vital to spiritual truth as taught by our Lord. There are certain artificial standards that some confuse with spiritual life and seek to impose on all Christians. Absurd

situations often arise when one is hard put in deciding what is right. For example, one artistic friend found herself working with Christians who considered color in clothing a mark of a worldly life and the wearing of white shoes on a hot day incompatible with a spiritual influence. The natural questions those non-conformists had to face was whether these offenses were causing others to stumble or whether there was a larger responsibility for straight thinking and discrimination between real and artificial standards that it was their duty to face courageously. It is often easier to give in for the sake of peace, but one is more likely to gain a permanent peace by facing the issue squarely and challenging such mental confusion of standards; this will help people in the end to a truer conception of those things that are worth dying for. There is a modern Pharisaism that "strains at a gnat and swallows a camel" that needs to be met in a fearless spirit of love. If some of those artificial standards can be put where they really belong, as the harmless personal fancies of individuals, we shall then be free to drive hard at those real ideals that ought to influence us all more powerfully than they do.

(4) *The Christian principle of voluntary sacrifice for others because of the example and expectation of our Lord should control a larger part of our conduct than it usually does.* "Hereby know we love, because he laid down his life for us; and we ought to lay down our lives for the brethren" (I John 3 : 16). It is good for us to practise the habit of self-discipline and self-restraint in matters of conduct in order that we may not become flabby in our moral muscle. The best cure for self-indulgence is voluntary sacrifice for Christ's sake. We need to conserve our vigor for large tasks and practise self-control in our conduct. There is ample motive for this so long as we live among people who are limited when we are free, who are in need when we have plenty. It is our privilege to make some real sacrifice that costs, for the sake of others. This ought often to decide matters of conduct about which we may be in doubt. Even if it be right to follow a given course, it may be best to forego it for the toning up of our moral fibre.

III. The principles of conduct that underlie our working together with God.

(1) *The purpose of our life determines a large part of our conduct.* Certain things that are good in themselves may become wrong for us if they hinder our larger purpose. A sense of responsibility for a task puts us on our honor to do our best work. This may mean the giving up of certain things in order that our purpose may be carried out. What may be right for my friend may be wrong for me because of the end I have chosen to attain. Every purpose requires concentration and the narrowing of interests for the time being, and it is well worth while, just because we may not do everything we can do, to sketch our purpose in vivid outline. This would not involve merely the purpose of a day or a month, but the perspective of a series of years; we can then fill in the days with purposes that will round out our objective so that life will have sequence and meaning and not be a series of unrelated acts.

(2) *If we have the perspective of a life which is consciously following the unfolding of God's purpose our scale of values will be changed.* This will settle many questions of conduct. Among the possible choices are some that have an abiding value in life; in the larger horizon they assume more importance. For example, a friendship may be difficult and cause one to debate the possible course of action. If one looks at the friendship as a transient experience of a year or two it will not seem worth while to perpetuate it, and one may let it go deliberately. But if one looks at a friendship as the beginning of an endless union leading up to God Himself, then in the perspective of the eternal life it is worth while to decide on conduct that will unfold and deepen the heart of friendship, realizing that our relationships here are the beginning of timeless bonds. Thus our relation to God brings us to see everything from His point of view and may lead us to do more than others may think necessary in faithfulness to our personal relationships.

As we keep all these principles in our minds and make them our rule of faith and practice we find it easier to make wise decisions about what we will or will not do, easier to find freedom for our spirits to grow. There are many people who prefer to live in a world that is catalogued; where everything has a label telling precisely what is "right" and what is "wrong." It is quite possible to live happily this way if one is a little child mentally, or if one does not want to think because of laziness, or overcaution, or fear of venturing. If one can trust implicitly some wise man to do the thinking and make rules with authority, life becomes simple, and it would have to stay simple, devoid of all the outreach of spirit and tangle of human wills that makes this world interesting. But if we are going to read many books, and rub up against many people, and if we yearn for the big world of life, there will be gaps unfilled by rules, and a conflict of authority that will in the end drive us back to Jesus Christ as our only authority. As we search His teachings we shall find principles but no rules, and we shall find that He trusts us to apply those principles to conduct. His big conflict with the Pharisees was the effort to guide them by principles when they insisted on having inflexible rules. The secret of character is inner control instead of outer authority.

People look at the details of our conduct and judge our character by the precise, habitual translation of our inner principles into outer life. They are drawn or repelled by the kind of character translation they see. Their trust in us helps us to express our ideals better and our expression inspires them to like ideals. Thus character becomes contagious through conduct and conduct alone produces character.

BIBLE STUDY XIV
Christian Conduct

I. *The secret of growth in character.*

Read II Cor. 3 : 17-18; II Peter 3 : 18; Phil. 3 : 12-14. Notice in each of these passages the sense of a time element, a process, and a growth in the making of a character. The spur to growth is found in the personal association with Jesus Christ, who makes us long to be like Him. Love is the greatest transforming power, and the "love of Christ constraineth us" until we are transformed into His likeness. When we make it our ambition to please Christ so that there is, each day, an honest obedience to His teaching we have the secret of a moral dynamic that works out in us a character that is consonant with our belief.

II. *Standards that are a guide for Christian conduct.*

(1) Read I Cor. 6 : 12 and Gal. 5 : 1. We must preserve the glorious freedom of the Spirit. In these passages Paul combats the pagan teaching of expediency which would allow indulgence so long as it did not get beyond certain limits. This same teaching has been promoted by many undiscerning Christians to-day in such words as "It is all right to follow

your desires for pleasure and indulgence, but be discreet enough to stop in time; do not overdo the matter, for it would not be expedient for your health and influence." On the other hand, Paul exclaims: "Do you say that all things are lawful but not all things are expedient? Yes, all things are lawful, but *I will not be brought under the power of any.*" The teaching of expediency says: "Follow your desires," but the freedom of the Spirit says that our desires must be held captive by the one great desire, viz.: that in all things Jesus Christ shall reign; that He must have everything in His control; and that we dare not give up our freedom in Him to follow anything else. Everything may be lawful, but does it interfere with our freedom in Him? Pleasure then becomes not a desire or end in itself, but a means of fitting us for a better service of Christ. How would this principle sift our pleasures if we applied it to our daily conduct?

Questions

Am I under the power of any self-indulgence? Do the things that I like to do weaken or strengthen my appreciation of the things of the Spirit?

(2) Read I Tim. 4 : 4 and Titus 1 : 15. Here we see the principle of *judging a thing to be right or wrong according to the purity of the Spirit.* It isn't the thing itself that is wrong but the use to which it is put. The question to be asked is whether a given thing ministers to self-destruction or to God's glory. The more the purifying stream of God's life flows through our hearts, the more our conscience and mind will be so cleansed that we will look upon the world with pure eyes, seeing all things pure. When our minds are not clean everything takes on the color of our own impure mind and becomes to us actually impure.

Questions

Would it be desirable, if possible, to remove everything that tempts the human spirit? What is it that leads us into temptation? See James 1 : 13, 14. What is the relation between thanksgiving and prayer and the decision about whether a thing is good for us, I Tim. 4 : 4. What kinds of things are smirched for us? Is it because of their inherent evil, or have they taken on the color of our thoughts? What am I doing, and what might I do to enlarge the horizon of purity around my life?

(3) Read I Cor. 8 : 1–13. *Conduct is based not on knowledge but on love that buildeth.* See Isaiah 58 : 10–12 for the vocation of the Christian in relationships with others.

Questions

How does Paul discuss the relative values of pleasures in I Cor. 8 : 13? When does a pleasure cease to be a pleasure? What determines our desires to follow certain lines of conduct? What causes desires to change? What is the appeal to our ambition and purpose in Isaiah 48 : 12? Does this appeal to serve others really govern my choices of what I will do?

(4) Read I Cor. 9 : 19 and Matt. 16 : 24, 25. *Our manner of living ought to be determined by the necessity of carrying out our share of the work of winning others to Christ.* Is any Christian exempt from the call to sacrifice for the sake of Jesus Christ? How would this affect our daily conduct if we believed this to be a test of whether we were truly following Christ? What am I doing for others that means a real laying down of life?

(5) Read I Cor. 9 : 22–24. *The fear lest we fail our Lord ought to guide us in some of our conduct.* Is it possible to inspire others to a life that we fail to enter ourselves? When are we most likely to fail? What relation has self-discipline and self-control with the victory of our spirit?

III. *Ourselves and others.*

Having settled the principles of the inner life it remains to be said that just as the upbuilding of others is to be the objective so the upbuilding of ourselves to be more efficient, skilled workmen for God is a legitimate objective provided that a balance is preserved between both. We can ask *all* things not alone for others, but for ourselves, in order to glorify our Lord better.

CHAPTER XV

THE APPROACH TO THOSE WHO LIVE AN UNBALANCED LIFE

One of the greatest hindrances to the progress of the kingdom among non-Christians comes from the unsymmetrical lives of Christians who present a deformed, distorted Christ to the world. Most of us personify the caricature instead of the character of Jesus Christ. There are a few features emphasized out of proportion to the others, and the result is a reflection upon the perfection of the Christian life.

It is important that we help those who are living an unbalanced Christian life, for they are usually unhappy and discontented either because they are conscious of their lack of balance or because they feel that others do not appreciate them. At the root there are usually these reasons why so many of us live unbalanced lives:

(1) *A lack of humility.* It is so easy to be content with our own point of view and the particular emphasis on truth that pleases us. We see things so distinctly that the very distinctness causes other objects to be blurred. We are satisfied with our own vision of truth and forget that no one individual can see all the truth at once. Our experiences in life, our inheritance, our temperament, our age, our work, our individual need have all in a large measure defined our point of view. We have such good reasons for believing ourselves to be right that we fail to see how others can have equally good reasons for believing themselves to be right. We shall always be unbalanced until we own to the truth that each of us sees "through a glass darkly," until we are willing to learn from others in humility. Then and only then can we begin to grow strong where we are weak and see where before we were blind.

(2) *A lack of horizon.* Each of us is a specialist, and rightly so. What we need is to see our specialty related to the whole. We work in our own little garden and have the worm's-eye view of every flower and shrub. It is only when we add

to this the bird's-eye view of our garden as it is related to the great landscape and the far-away stretches of horizon that we get a true perspective and balance. If we were to study the little habits of our life it would disclose our lack of horizon. When we talk only with people who agree with us, or read books that say what we have always thought, when we are critical of any new ideas before we have proved their value, or shut our ears to what others are saying because it opposes our notions, we are thereby limiting our power to find a permanent balance for our life.

(3) *A failure to co-ordinate all our experiences in Jesus Christ as the centre in whom " all things hold together."* It is in the universal personality of our Lord that we see the most perfect balance of all virtues and powers. His point of view is as wide as the world and eternity and in Him everything has its true emphasis and importance. If we studied the life of our Lord, appreciating the perfect symmetry of it, we would find it easier to keep from mental astigmatism and lopsidedness. We ought to challenge each new experience and point of view until we see how it co-ordinates with His life. If it does not fit into His pattern we can safely reject it; if it does fit we dare not go on without adding it to the expression of our Christian life.

It takes courage to face facts and look at ourselves in the light of the perfection of our Lord and then resolutely go to work to correct the thinking that is awry and disciplining our spirits in our weak points. But honesty and courage will solve more than half the problem, and the end is so to be desired that it is worth all the pain and cost.

The qualities of Christian character may be listed in these groups. There are those qualities that are inner and personal, there are others that develop through our relations with other individuals, and there are those that grow in us as an outcome of our relation to our community and generation. Under the personal qualities we include devoutness, purity, kindness, integrity, ambition, temperance, and patience. Under the head of our relationship with others we list forgiveness, intercession, sacrifice, influence, compassion. In the list of qualities of character that develop as a result of our relation to our community are included civic interest, the relief of suffering, Christian citizenship, revolt against injustice, and the succoring of the weak.

There are Christians who conceive of the Christian life as embracing but one group of these virtues. Their influence is weakened and ineffective because of this limitation, while the outside world of observers who realize in some dim way that Christ personified all these qualities expect the Christian to be like his Lord in this. We sometimes find people who are interested in others and eager to bring people to know Christ. They intercede in prayer and appeal to them, and yet they are so lacking in the personal gifts of patience, gentleness, or integrity that the appeal is valueless. It is as Emerson says: "What you *are* stands over you the while, and thunders so that I cannot hear what you say to the contrary."

Again, we see devout people of great integrity and purity of heart who are content with the refinements of personal Christian character and are indifferent to the claims of the community and the non-Christians whom they meet. They are so content with saving their own souls that they forget the needs of others. There is also another class of unbalanced Christians who see vividly the need of the community and stop content with reformation and the relief of injustice, yet are uninterested in personal devoutness and purity or in intercession for others that they may know the Christ.

Whenever any one deliberately denies expression to any of these three groups of qualities, the vision of the Christ is distorted and the fulness of the divine life is restrained. We are in sore need to-day of recognizing this lack of balance in life and, as honest Christians, we need to clear ourselves of this charge and help others to release new spiritual energies that the kingdom of our Lord may come more speedily.

But even more serious is the lack of balance that is present so often among the states of personal character: devoutness without clean lips and purity of action; integrity without patience and kindness and forgiveness; or purity and integrity without moderation or devoutness. It is here especially that we meet the question of personal influence over our friends and acquaintances, and we fail pitifully to win their respect for our Christian character by the lack of balance in the personal expression of our inner life.

We all see our need at this point but we want to know how we are going to help ourselves or others to transform this personal caricature of the inner Christian life into a true Christian character. What are the secrets of growth in grace until we attain more nearly unto "the measure of the stature of the fulness of Christ?"

In the first place, we need to become self-conscious in this matter. It would help us much if we listed all these qualities of character in a book and in the presence of God held a self-examination at regular seasons, asking ourselves where we have failed to manifest these marks of the Christian life. And, as we face our lack of balance in any particular way, we shall be able through intercession to develop a sensitiveness of spirit that will guard us from future shortcomings.

Fellowship with other Christians who are strong in the points where we are weak is a great stimulus to our own growth. Here is where we can enrich our lives by surrounding ourselves with many Christian friends each of whom can make a special contribution of strength to us. "Character," as has been said, "is caught, and not taught," and we need the fellowship with those who have highly contagious cases of the special personal qualities wherein we are lacking.

We also need a laboratory for demonstration purposes. Many of us wonder why we are so often surrounded by people who seem to call out just the opposite states of character which we know to be the fruit of the Spirit of God. They come into our horizon as test cases for the application of the very phase of character that we need. We grow strong only by the exercise of the little power we have. For example, we can only grow in the grace of forgiveness when we find in the laboratory of life some one who needs our forgiveness; integrity is best manifested when it is the positive reaction against some form of insincerity; devoutness only grows real when we have deliberately to choose it in the midst of an undevout companionship. And love becomes strong and deep not so much when it is the line of least resistance, because we are borne along by natural sympathy and congeniality, but when we must deliberately cultivate it by a decision of will whereby we determine to be considerate and tender and sacrificing, and trustful with those to whom we are not naturally drawn. All these personal states of Christian character must be deliberately shown toward those who do not naturally call out these spiritual energies; and we shall discover that the very resistance which we meet will develop spiritual vigor and a well-rounded life.

It is love itself that helps most in our efforts for balance. The wider our sympathies, the more people we take into our hearts, the more we will hunger and thirst to measure up to their expectations, so that we may not fail them in any way. In the same way we long not to disappoint God who loved us when we were unlovable and created in us the desire to be like Him.

In closing, there is one inner spirit that is necessary to all balance of life, and that is the spirit of self-discipline and self-control. We must learn to "endure hardness as good soldiers" and be willing to let the discipline of our spirits, in all those states where we are lacking, go on steadily. Every victory we win means new power to serve and a larger sphere of influence. It would be cheerless and difficult to hold ourselves to the spirit of discipline were it not balanced up by the other gifts of God, viz., power and love. Through God's power and through the realization of His unfailing love we can endure the struggle to discipline our spirits until the balanced life is not only a state of inner experience but an outshining character seen and read of all men.

BIBLE STUDY XV

A Well-Poised Life

Read II Tim. 1 : 7. The threefold gift of God to our life; power, love, and discipline. All three are needed to keep one in balance. Power that is not balanced by love is cruel and autocratic; love that is not strengthened by discipline becomes mere sentimentality. Discipline that is not balanced by power or love becomes useless and lifeless. Every Christian needs the blend of the three; and they are held in co-ordination only as they are controlled and developed by the Spirit of God.

(1) *Power*—our capacity for influence; all that goes to make up our assets in life; all our resources, and potential leadership. Some have so much that they are led away by it; some have so little that they are weakened. Read the account of two people who had great power not balanced by love and not controlled by God's Spirit. (*a*) Jezebel. Read I Kings 16 : 30, 31; ch. 18 : 13; ch. 19 : 1, 2; ch. 21 : 1–16. (*b*) Saul. Acts 7 : 58 to 8 : 3; ch. 9 : 1, 2. Read also the account of a man whose power was inadequate for a great test and yet who was able to do the humanly impossible thing when God's power controlled him. Luke 22 : 54–62 and Acts 2 : 14–24, 38–41. See also Acts 22 : 3–11; ch. 9 : 20–22. What is the secret of this transformation? See Phil. 2 : 13:

"It was said of —— that he always seemed a man of weak will but that an iron will seemed to be working through him."

(*Forbes Robinson.*)

AN UNBALANCED LIFE

See Eph. 3 : 20 for the assurance of God's power beyond all our asking. Therefore the message of Romans 12 : 1 and II Cor. 4 : 7 (see the Weymouth translation) is necessary for all of us who would be well poised in our power; otherwise our power becomes dangerous.

(2) *Love.*—Read I Cor. 13 for the description of the active energy of love. Love is not a feeling or emotion merely, but an active will toward another manifesting itself in voluntary self-sacrifice for another's good. The pleasure and emotion in love is dependent on the response to the purpose of the one who loves and the appreciation of the cost of self-sacrifice.

Read Luke 9 : 40–50. What is it that called out the love of this woman? Read I John 3 : 14–18. How do we recognize love in God? Can there be true love apart from the principle of sacrifice?

Love attains its purity and power only as it is selfless; it becomes selfless when it is controlled by God. Therefore, love, too, can only be poised when it finds its centre outside of itself—in God and in others.

(3) *Discipline.*—Self-indulgence may be conquered in two ways: by abstinence and by self-control. Self-control is more difficult than abstinence. Read Matt. 18 : 8–10. Here our Lord indicates the principle of abstinence as far better than losing one's life. Abstinence from a known evil is always necessary but self-control is needed in the use of legitimate things. Abstinence in legitimate things is often necessary for the sake of proving to ourselves that we are not under the power of anything.

Read I Cor. 9 : 19, 25–27. Here discipline and self-control are the means by which the *purpose* is attained. It is because of the goal, "that I may attain," that we pay the price of discipline.

Read I Tim. 4 : 7, last clause. Discipline is for the purpose of building up reserve power and moral muscle. God pity the man or woman who has no goal or purpose in life that makes "enduring hardness" worth while! Discipline is only valuable as it reinforces power and love; it does not become an end in itself.

CHAPTER XVI

THE APPROACH TO THOSE WHO ARE FEELING AFTER REALITY

There is a growing hunger in the heart of most people who are thinking about their religious needs. They insist that reality shall be the touchstone for all their thinking. "God is not real to me; how does He become so to any one?" is a question often asked. If ever there was an age in which people were unwilling to accept spiritual truth merely because some authority says that it is true, this is the age. They insist upon finding the core of reality before they believe and, like Thomas of old, want to put their fingers on the very nail-prints in the hands of their Master before they can say: "My Lord and my God." Unlike our Lord, we are often impatient with this quest and do not take the time to show these would-be disciples how to find the kind of evidence they require.

At the outset we need to remind ourselves that all of us started out in life with a capacity for God and for spiritual reality. As little children the unseen spiritual mysteries were more real than the external world about us, but it became increasingly difficult to hold the vision of them as material things began to absorb our attention. The world became full of distracting "things," and the single eye of the heart could not compete with the thousand eyes of the mind. But we never forgot what we had once realized and we have thirsted to find it again. We discover that spiritual reality is like the reality of music. We may be born with an ear for it, but we all know that it takes more than an ear for music to make it a great reality in our life. It is the prize awarded to a disciplined life. Let us look at some of the tests by which we find reality in anything.

(1) *Reality depends upon attention*. We enter a room filled with lovely things; our attention is held by a bowl of nasturtiums on a table. It recalls a friend's garden, our comradeship,

and love and joy in the relation with that friend, and although we sit there in that room in the body, we are dead to it all; for we are living in the spirit and in the realities of life as our attention is held by that bowl of flowers. Now, if anything so simple as a flower brings reality to our spirit when we fix our attention on it, how much more could the things of life and the spirit become vivid if we let Jesus Christ hold our attention. Only that part of life to which we attend is ever real. Perhaps if we recall our Lord to our mind that act alone will make Him real.

(2) *Time also brings reality.* A great friend quietly slipped away into God's presence before any one suspected the possibility of it. For days afterward her fellow workers said to one another: "I know that she is gone but I cannot realize it." But as time went on and as the many services she had given had to be taken on by others, and the gaps that were left came to light, the reality of her going became a fact of consciousness that brought a greater ache of heart as the days went by. They not only knew that she had gone but they felt it and realized it. So it is with our experience with God. It takes time to realize how all our life is empty without Him and it also takes time to realize how fully He slips into our lives and becomes interwoven with all our experiences. It may help us to find Him real if we look back into the years and remember all the ways in which we have felt His touch on our lives. "I girded thee, even though thou didst not know me," is the word that came to the people of old, and it is just as true to-day. He will become real as we take time to let Him make Himself a real part of our continued experiences.

(3) *A fact becomes real in proportion to our understanding of it.* Perhaps this may have been illustrated in our experience as it was in the case of one woman. She had bought goods for years in a large shop where the saleswomen were to her no more than so many automatic hands to take down goods from the shelves. One day she came to know, through her church work, the struggles of one of these girls to support her invalid mother. As she began to understand the problems of this one girl, she discovered that the next time she entered the shop the faces of all the saleswomen began to stand out in vivid reality, and she almost forgot her business in wondering how many others were having the same economic struggle. In the same way

other things in life grow real as we come to understand them. It is equally true in spiritual as well as material matters. God becomes real as we come to know and understand His character and will through a continued study of His revealed truth. "Then shall we know if we follow on to know the Lord."

(4) *Reality depends upon the use we make of anything.* The more a material thing or any interest of our life fits into our daily need the more vivid it becomes. The friend to whom we scarcely ever write or whom we rarely see tends to disappear from our consciousness. We get along so easily without that comradeship that our sense of reality grows dim. Many people do not find God real because they get along so easily without Him and do not include Him as an indispensable part of their daily life. They hear Him spoken of on Sunday but never take Him into account in their business and plans and thinking. He can never reveal Himself until they make a place for Him which is empty unless He fills it. Then He becomes real.

(5) *Love also brings reality.* It is like the developing fluid which brings out the clear outlines of the picture on the dull film. The things we care for most are the things we always notice. An artist who loves beauty sees it clearly wherever he goes; the woman who loves babies always sees them first in a crowd. To the lover, his friend is the one outstanding figure. To the one who loves a clean heart and truth and perfection, God grows vivid as the centre and source of it all. Perhaps the reason why some people cannot find God real is that they do not have pure desires and do not hunger and thirst after righteousness.

(6) *The absence of what we desire may make it real.* A little boy on a ferry-boat was absorbed with delight at the sight of the shipping in the harbor. He ventured away from his mother and the other children to see the sights on the river. Soon the boat stopped and the people started to go. Suddenly the wailing voice of the boy cried: "Where's my *mother!*" But she was close behind him and soon became joyously real to him—real in a way that she had not been a few minutes before when he was occupied with ships. So it is with many who want to find God. He is at hand all the time, waiting to reveal Himself; but, absorbed in other things, His children wander off until some change in circumstances creates a sense of apprehension and the cry "Where is my God!" comes involuntarily. This experience

ought to prove to them that the very cry indicates that He is in the background of their lives if they will but turn and look to Him.

One of the common mistakes people make in seeking reality is to confuse it with the sense of feeling. They want to *feel* near God, to *feel* His strength, to *feel* His companionship. If they stop to think, however, they will soon see that feeling plays a very uncertain rôle in our life and is not to be relied on as a true test of reality. Feeling is often uncontrollable; it sweeps over us like a tempest and then is gone. We may feel kindly toward a person one day and feel critical toward the same person the next day. Our temperature of feeling goes up and down with the weather, with our health, and with our temperamental quirks. So used are we to the freaks of feeling that we do our work without reference to it; if we did not, most of us would do little.

We get rest only when we see that reality is not dependent on feeling alone but on willing and knowing. The last two are necessities; the first is a luxury. I first must know my friend as a fact of experience; I must also be willing to be related to that friend; I may feel a joy in the friendship but it cannot last or be real unless the knowing and willing are the foundations of the relationship.

It is so with our relation to God. I must know Him as a fact of my experience and know Him in His true character and purposes toward me. Then I must be willing to relate myself to Him in obedience and friendship. Then He is a reality in my life whether I *feel* Him to be so or not.

In the last analysis, the chief reason why God is not real to some people is the fact of their moral blindness. It is the "pure in heart" that have no difficulty in seeing God; it is our sins that "have hidden His face from us"; it is disobedience to His word that cuts us off from fellowship with Him. Unconfessed sin, unwillingness to put our daily life under the holy scrutiny of God, are like the "earth-born clouds" that rise to hide Him from our eyes. As surely as we face these causes and remove them, just so surely will God become vivid and real to our hearts.

BIBLE STUDY XVI

The Search for Reality

I. Read II Cor. 4 : 1–6. God becomes real as we see Him in the face of Jesus Christ. Through contact with the historic person of Christ we discern God. John 14 : 8–9 satisfies our desire to know what God is like. What reason is given in II Cor. 4 : 3, 4 why the image of God is hidden from the minds of people? If God seems dim and far away, let us get a close look at Jesus Christ.

II. Read Luke 24 : 25–27 and John 5 : 39, 40. God becomes real as we study the scriptures. Chinese Gordon said: "In times of coldness, when Christ recedes, I spend time on the writings and He becomes vivid and real." This will prove true for all of us as we open the mind and heart to the teachings. They find us in our conscience, and we know in the depths of our Spirit that we are face to face with God. The habit of recalling some word of Christ during the day often brings Him near so that He seems to be speaking to us with the intimacy of a friend.

III. Read John 16 : 13, 14, and Heb. 3 : 7, 8, also Rev. 3 : 20. We find reality in the voice of God speaking to our conscience. Sometimes it is the inner prompting that makes us conscious of Him, and often it is the working out of circumstances or the illumination which comes from others. There are times when we find the words of Isaiah 45 : 5 as true of us as they were of Cyrus, and discover that God has laid his hand on us even when we did not know it. How many times we have been baffled in our thinking and at our wit's end, and then found help through some flash of light that lit up the truth for us and gave us the needed wisdom!

IV. Read John 14 : 21 and John 7 : 17. We discover God to be real in proportion as we enter into real dealings with Him and yield our will in obedience to His teaching. When we face the struggle of the soul that precedes a harmonizing of our will with His will, we soon gain a vivid experience with God. The doing makes the thinking real. People who are uncongenial do not discern one another, largely because of conflicting desires and tastes and wills. So it is with God; we discern Him only as we become one with Him.

V. Matt. 5 : 8; Psalm 24 : 4; Matt. 17 : 2; I Tim. 1 : 5; and II Tim. 2 : 22. God dwells in all purity and light and it is only the pure in heart who do see Him. It is not for the one who does not pay this price to say that God is not real. We must not swerve from our hatred of sin in all its forms if we would have God increasingly real to us. It is the one who loves beauty who actually sees beauty. There is no use in trying to convince some one who has no love for music that a sonata is beautiful; it must be in the heart first.

VI. Matt. 28 : 19, 20; 25 : 31–46. We find God in reality as we seek Him among those who need Him. The promise of His presence is given to those who are carrying the word of life to those who have not heard. It is doing this "unto the least of them" that helps us to find Him.

THE SEARCH FOR REALITY 137

"The healing of His seamless dress
Is by our beds of pain
We touch Him in life's throng and press
And we are whole again."

(Whittier.)

Questions for Thought

What do I call real? Is it something I can picture or something I can feel or something that I know as a fact? Is faith a help to reality? In what way? Why does anything seem to become more real if we share it with some one else? Why are feelings unreliable evidences of reality? What are the surest evidences?

CHAPTER XVII

DEVELOPING THE RELIGIOUS LIFE OF CHILDREN

Most of us ought to have some of our richest opportunities for service in dealing with the religious life of children. They are with us in our homes, in school, and in the church, and respond so quickly to our personal interest in them when we take the pains really to know them and appreciate them.

It takes an unusually genuine spirit to help children to know God. There are no more searching tests applied to our spiritual life than those administered by children who instinctively read our hearts; and it is because of our failure to meet these tests that we feel ourselves so often self-conscious and *gauche* in their presence. There are certain conditions that must be met if we would guide children spiritually.

First and all the time we must be utterly *natural*. Any suggestion of an artificial manner repels at once. When speaking about spiritual realities a change of voice to a solemn and sepulchral tone, unlike the tones we would use in speaking of some every-day affair, is quickly detected, and the small boy or girl retires behind an impenetrable mask beyond reach of our influence. Children are so near to the kingdom of God that they think as naturally about spiritual matters as they do about material affairs, and an air of assumed constraint makes them conscious of an unpleasant lump somewhere within them and they want to run.

They also demand reality. Any trace of cant is felt at once. It is only the spontaneous life of the heart that wins children. They want to know about living things and people and they want to know the truth. There is a vein of scepticism in the minds of most children that challenges statements or silently watches to see if statement and fact tally. Most of us have at least a partial remembrance of the eagle eye with which we used to watch grown folk and make our quiet discoveries and draw our crude conclusions. There were a few honest spirits who spoke with crystal sincerity and dealt with us as real persons and we accepted them at once. Woe betide any one who cannot meet the eager direct look of a little child with the same frankness.

A fine courtesy is also needed if we would win children. They are so aware of difference in size and age between them and us that they appreciate deeply the same respect for personality that we would show toward grown-ups. We little know what enduring pain we inflict on children when, for example, we laugh over their mistakes in the presence of others and ridicule their opinions as we would not dare ridicule the foolish talk of adults. Discourtesy kills childlike trust and contradicts the spirit of love.

One must also have confidence in children if one would understand their spiritual life. There are rare gifts of the spirit that are the unconscious part of a child's religion, which we sophisticated grown folk might well envy. We need to see that the teaching is not all on our side; that the little ones can teach us if we are humble and that we can trust their spiritual instincts. Our confidence must be based on an appreciation of what we can count upon in them. Directness, faith, a sense of justice, simplicity of motive, spontaneous response to the ideal, an intense consciousness of God's personality, eagerness to "do something"—surely these are some of the marks of a child's spiritual life on which we can build character and find a basis for real comradeship.

We will not get far in our work with children unless we have a childlike heart; not the condescending spirit that hopes to make an impression by childish imitations, or "talks down" to them, but that which comes from a real appreciation of a child's point of view and a joy in its companionship. It will do us good to revise our vocabulary and learn to say deep things in simple, one-syllable words. If we have this childlike heart we will also be free from sentimentality, which healthy-minded children resent. The reason that many of them usually prefer men to women is probably due to the fact that women so often make children feel conspicuous by their sentimental and personal remarks, whereas men are more matter of fact. There is nothing that embarrasses the ordinary child more than to be made to feel conspicuous.

There are certain foundation-stones which should underlie

the spiritual character-building of children up to their early adolescence. Many of the difficulties of older youth would melt away if the early influences were what they should be.

The first of these elemental needs concerns a *true conception of God*. He should be spoken of as a heavenly Father, who once revealed Himself to men in the person of Jesus Christ so that all people might know what He is like; that He has infinite power, infinite love, and infinite wisdom and holiness; that He made us and keeps us in life and wants us all to be like Him in our hearts. It is better to guide the imagination about what God our Father is like by the stories of what Jesus Christ said and did and by resemblances of God which an earthly father may show than by the inadequate conceptions of mediæval art and pictures on charts. Many an older student often turns away from the thought of a personal God because of the limited attempts of art to picture Him. It is sad indeed when children have no experience of noble earthly fatherhood to supply concrete expression to their conception of God. In such cases the vision of Jesus Christ must be given all the more vividness and reality.

The spirit of love can be developed by the stories of the love of Jesus Christ toward sick folk, lepers, and blind men, and by teaching of His love of nature, of flowers and birds and everything that God has made. The child needs to be helped to express it through definite thankfulness and gratitude for all the ways in which the heavenly Father ministers to us. The habit of giving thanks each day for the new ways in which God's love has been discovered is one of the most important factors in helping a child to a real appreciation of the true character of God. In addition to the sense of God's love and care, great emphasis should be placed on the expectation of God that we should be right in heart, word, and deed and thought. He is the only One who can make and keep the heart clean. As children are learning the clear-cut distinctions between right and wrong in their daily experience their sensitiveness to a broken fellowship is keen. They know that they have need of a restored sense of oneness with God and the feeling that He is pleased with them. Their experience is confined to definite wrongdoings which lie heavy on their sensitive consciences, and often the first real experience of God's nearness comes when they confess their faults to Him and ask forgiveness. Just here it should be emphasized that children should be taught the need and value of confession of wrong-doing, for in no way can the education of the will for right choices be better secured. Many a child bears a weight that haunts it by night simply because it has not been helped to make a clean breast of it and enter into the relief of a sense of forgiving love.

It is also necessary that the religious programme of children should concentrate on storing their minds with Bible facts, stories, and teachings. At the age of twenty a beautiful girl became blind. During the days of depression that followed she said: "I wish I had some comfort from my religion, but somehow my mind seems so empty. I can recall endless poems and Mother Goose rhymes and nature stories, but they don't help me now. Why didn't my teachers teach me Psalms and the sayings of Jesus Christ instead of those things? That is what I need now." She was indeed right. How can we expect to have the strength of God for all the testings and exigencies of life if our minds do not become a storehouse of God's teachings so that His spirit may be able to fulfil that promise of our Lord that He would bring to our remembrance those things that He has said to us. The Bible is so rich in story lore and simple teaching that no child ought to be defrauded of the inheritance of moral strength and ideals and fellowship with Jesus Christ which comes from storing the mind with the words of the Bible. Nothing can equal the importance of this duty toward children if we ever expect them to have moral fibre and the ideals of Jesus Christ.

In building up a Christian character in children we should teach them a great reverence for facts and the difference between a right and wrong use of the imagination. Much of the scepticism of early youth grows out of the shock of discovering that one's father or mother or teacher had proved untrustworthy in saying that fairy-tales were so when they *weren't* so. This is pre-eminently an age of reality when we are facing a type of child unknown to the past generation. The modern child through the "motion-picture" habit and the blatant realism of newspapers and magazines and popular books becomes sophisticated at a tender age and develops a subtle cynicism that has to be met with entire truthfulness on the part of any one who would teach him. A reverence for truth and trust in a truthful teacher who does not fail will do much to correct the difficulties arising from suspicion later on. The joys of the imaginative life of children will be no less if they are taught the difference between what they see with the eyes of their mind and the eyes of their body. And they can be helped, too, to use their imaginations to think about things that are really true, and the mental pictures of Jesus Christ that can be created from the facts of His life, and the remembrance of beautiful and true experiences that have come into their life with people and things. All of this is a solemn obligation when we realize that we are dealing with the very foundation of character, and the basic distinctions between right and wrong—between sincerity and insincerity, and are responsible to our God, "with whom there is no variableness" and who "desireth truth in the inward parts." We owe it to every child to help it to live a life of utter truthfulness.

Another indispensable element in the religious life of children is the spirit of obedience, not as an end in itself but as a means of co-operating with others for a common good. Fortunate are those little ones who learn it from loving parents; but there are abounding evidences that countless children never are taught obedience in their homes and so have no reverence toward God. Therefore the teacher has to help the child to see how everything in nature and life is held by the law of co-operation and how our highest happiness and perfection come only as we yield obedience to Jesus Christ. In proportion as children learn to love God they will want increasingly to please Him, but in the beginning they need to learn that love is only expressed and developed through a cheerful yielding to the will of love. It is as our Lord said: "He that hath my commandments and keepeth them he it is that loveth me." Children must be helped to see that disobedience destroys the loving relationship with their Father and makes it impossible for them to know Him. There are scores of analogies in daily experience that prove this: for instance, a child can never know how to play a piano unless it obeys the words of direction that are given it by the teacher. Obedience is the gateway to knowledge and power. It is the basis of all that reverence for God that will hold the child true in its later life.

The characteristic of all youth is boundless energy and the desire to "do things"; therefore service for God is an indispensable part of a child's religious life. We need to help children to see the possibilities for personal and group service by which they can follow in the steps of Jesus Christ. The "cup of cold water" given out of love for Him is typical of countless personal services that children may give with the Spirit of Christ to those in their homes or at school. Opportunities to serve as a group can be provided through work done by a class to earn money for missions, or by some united service for the church and Sunday-school, or for the poor in the parish. The essential part is the personal gift of strength and time and money and effort that alone makes service a genuine expression of a child's Christian life.

We must help children, too, to understand the real value of prayer and give them wise guidance about coming to God with the desires of their hearts. Otherwise we may be faced some day by a child who will say to us what a small boy said one night to his mother when he had finished his bedtime prayer. Looking steadily into the eyes of his mother, he announced: "Mother, I don't believe there's anything in this business of prayer." It was not till then that she realized how inadequate her teaching had been. Children should be taught to come to their heavenly Father simply and naturally to thank Him for His care and the joys of the day and for all the gifts of His love. Thankfulness leads to reverence. They need also to ask His help in doing what is right, in speaking the truth, in obeying willingly, in doing faithful work, in conquering ill temper, and in making right the wrong-doings that are on their consciences. If they could be helped thus early to go to God for spiritual gifts there would be a growing life of real understanding with God. They can be led to trust God's care, that He will provide for their needs through their parents or through other friends and that He gives us all the privilege of sharing our good things with others. Prayer can be a means of teaching unselfishness and thoughtfulness for others rather than an eager petitioning for selfish desires. If not a sparrow falls to the ground unnoticed by the heavenly Father, surely the children may come to Him with all the thoughts and needs of their hearts and speak them out to Him in full confidence that He will understand and help. "Suffer the little children to come unto me, and forbid them not, for of such is the kingdom of heaven."

BIBLE STUDY XVII
Christ's Teaching about Children

Read Matt. 19 : 13-15. Do not defraud any little child of its right to come to Jesus Christ, for it instinctively understands the spirit of the kingdom of heaven. Do not wait until it has grown puzzled about life and feels the first sense of loneliness and of being misunderstood. Help every little child to be conscious of its heavenly Father's presence and love. We need to remember that the heart of religion is the sense of relationship to God issuing in a spirit of trust and the unresisting will; all this, which will be natural to a child, we grown folk so often struggle to attain. The battles of adult life will be easier if the children have experienced the blessing of Christ.

Read Matt. 18 : 1-14. The teaching of Jesus Christ is explicit. It is the child spirit in us that wins our entrance into the kingdom, verses 3-4. Many of us have learned to become as little children as we have lived with them. We must ourselves live toward our heavenly Father in the same spirit of humble dependence and simple directness; and with the same eagerness to enter into life and make discoveries. We need to pray often the words of that old hymn:

> "As a little child relies
> On a care beyond his own;
> Knows he's neither strong nor wise;
> Fears to take one step alone:
> Thus let me with Thee abide
> As my Father, Friend, and Guide."

In verse 5 and in Mark 9 : 36, 37 the test is applied to us. Is the spirit of our Lord so truly in our hearts that we can receive a little child in His name, or have we grown so far away from simplicity that we find nothing in common between us? If we discover that we cannot honestly "receive" a child, we would better examine our hearts and see if we ourselves are living consciously and trustfully as children of our Father. It would lift our Christianity out of the confusion of theological differences into the realm of real fellowship with God; and people would discover their Father.

In verses 6-9. The test Jesus applies to us is more severe. He uses the strongest figure He can summon to warn us against the sin of causing "*one*" little one "to stumble." Every child has the right to live in the closest fellowship with his heavenly Father, and our supreme service to God is so to live that we will make it easy for any child to find his Father. How would our life have to be changed in its conversation, spirit, and daily influence if we applied to our hearts this solemn warning of Jesus Christ? Are there barriers in our interpretations of Jesus' teachings, in the inconsistencies of our lives, and in our indifferent spirit that baffle any child that is trying to find God?

Read verse 10 in the light of the preceding verses. Here the challenge of our Lord applies to every little one in the world, even those who seem beyond the circle of our sympathies. We are not to despise one of these little ones, because they are so close and dear to our Father. The verses that follow, 11–14, reveal the very heart of God as He seeks out the one who has gone astray. It is not sufficient that the little one be not despised—we must do more than that: we must seek, even at great cost, the one child who has missed the way. It is not easy to read this teaching of Jesus and continue to live and think as we have done in the past. Perchance we shall find it true of us as it was of the Pharisees to whom our Lord said: "Ye shut the kingdom of heaven against men: for ye enter not in yourselves, neither suffer ye them that are entering in to enter" (Matt. 23 : 13).

Questions for Thought

How do I know I have entered the kingdom of heaven? Have I met the test of becoming "as little children"? How does my attitude toward children and sympathy for their religious life prove this?

CHAPTER XVIII

THE SOURCES OF GROWTH

Every normal Christian life is a growing life. When the roots of life are centred in Jesus Christ there should be no limit to the possible capacity for Christian thinking and living. When our Lord said, "I am come that they may have life and may have it abundantly," He not only meant eternal length of life, but depth of life which would release all the hidden powers of personality, and breadth of life which would make us kin to the whole world in sympathy and appreciation; He meant also height of life which would lift us up from sordid thoughts to limitless reaches of heavenly wisdom. Therefore, when once the decision has been made that in all things Jesus Christ shall have the foremost place in the heart, the will in obedience to God works out His purposes in daily Christian living. Every spiritual impression requires a corresponding expression. Every inspiration toward loyalty to Christ should issue in some forward step.

There are certain ways in which the Christian life naturally expresses itself and connects itself with sources of growth. Chief amongst these is the open confession of Christ as Redeemer and King through the union with His body, the church. Although some people think it is possible to live a Christian life without becoming a member of the church visible, such an attitude is contrary to the teaching of the disciples of our Lord and the counsel of our Lord Himself. He asks for open, fearless loyalty to Him by confessing Him before men: "Every one therefore who shall confess me before men, him will I also confess before my Father who is in heaven" (Matt. 10 : 32). And the church is the body of believers in Christ who stand before the world as a witness to His kingship and redemption. Our Lord's prayer that all His own should be one in Him gives deep significance to His church.

Likewise, we cannot lightly disregard the solemn obligations of baptism and the Holy Communion. Too often in this age of excessive individualism some are prone to regard the church as a human organization or club of which they may become a part or not according to personal likes or dislikes of ministers, members, or services. We must help them to see that the church is made up of imperfect people like themselves who need worship and praise and inspiration. It is reasonable to infer that this help will come in greater measure through the corporate life of the church than from any group outside who are not openly loyal to Christ. Samuel Johnson voiced this truly when he said: "To be of no church is dangerous. Religion, of which the rewards are distant, and which is animated only by faith and hope, will glide by degrees out of the mind unless it be invigorated and reimpressed by external ordinances, by stated calls to worship, and the salutary influence of example."

It is usually best to unite with that branch of the church with which one has been most closely associated from childhood. If there are no such associations, we should counsel those who have decided to be Christians to relate themselves to that denomination in which they find the largest opportunities for worship, service, and loyalty to Christ.

Every Christian needs also the reinforcement of Christian friendships. It is one of the wonderful ways in which God completes our life and helps us to understand the fulness of His character as we see different reflections of it in the hearts of His friends. All Christians need two kinds of friends: they need to feel a sense of responsibility for some younger or weaker Christians who need their strength and help; they also need friendships with those from whom they can get spiritual stimulus. We need not only to hold others to their best but also to be held to our best by others. Christian friendships are potent factors in our experiences. They help us to grow in reverence, humility, self-denial, loyalty, self-forgetfulness, and patience. The spirit of friendliness toward others is one of the marks of the spirit of Christ.

The logical outcome of the spirit of friendliness in the Christian is the development of a social consciousness and sense of obligation to others. This ought inevitably to lead to some form of Christian service for the church, the community, and the individual. We shall not have done all we should to help until we guide young Christians to some definite form of service that will enlist all their powers. The call to service might well be voiced in those words: "I expect to pass through this world but once. Any good that I can do or any kindness that I can show let me do it now; let me not neglect or defer it, for I shall not pass this way again."

The average church member needs to be shown the many natural outlets for service that are possible. They need to see the daily opportunity for Christian service through their homes in being true to all those who come to their doors. There are countless maids and seamstresses, laundresses and porters, children and visitors who could be won to a Christian life if the average Christian woman obeyed her call to service. We must not only be good but we must be good for something and be a channel for God's life-giving power.

As time goes on the desire will come to form some definite purpose for service whereby one's brief life here can count most for the kingdom. The purposeful Christian will not go on drifting from one daily incident to another, but will shape plans toward some great objective and find out God's purpose for the life. This discovery may send loyal Christians into their own homes to live there according to the will of God; it may send them out to teach, to engage in business, to the professional service in philanthropic or religious work, or it may carry them into the life of a foreign missionary. The work is incidental; the discovery of our special place in the will of God is essential.

We shall not have done all that we can for young Christians unless we have helped them to some simple working method of Bible study that will feed the springs of their spiritual life. Bible classes and courses are essential for most people, to give direction and background to their religious thinking, but they can never take the place of the private study of the Bible which presses its claim on the conscience and reveals the thoughts and intents of the heart. If the Bible is taken as a library of books, each book having been written for certain occasions, people, and purposes, it will repay the thoughtful reader if it is studied book by book with an intelligent appreciation of the special message each was meant to convey. We need to help people to find something more than moral precepts in the Bible; to feel the throbbing message of the writer in all its entirety and to trace the way the message of God to men won its way in spite of obstacles and prejudices of men. It is the wonderful record of humanity's experiences with God, and every Christian experience to-day needs the guide-posts and stimulus and c   tive of the teaching of the Bible. It is the chief way, too, in which the personality of our Lord can be kept vivid and compelling in our hearts.

The reality of our personal experiences with God becomes vivid when we express them in our relationships with people. We possess for ourselves only what we share. As Doctor Coe remarks: "Social communion is the very experience which gives the 'me' any meaning at all" (Coe, *Psychology of Religion*, p. 198). It is as we realize some one else to whom our life must be related in love that we grow conscious of our own self-expression. As the teaching runs: "We *know* that *we* have passed from death into life, because we love the *brethren*." "He that loveth not abideth in death" (I John 3 : 14). Every Christian, therefore, who is eager to have an increasingly conscious fellowship with God must find some way of sharing his fellowship with others, or, rather, must expect to find this fellowship with God vivid through loving regard for others. A college girl who had recently given God, consciously, the control of her life was asked by a friend what it meant to be a Christian. As she shared her experience with an affectionate plea that her friend should not miss the possibility of having a similar joy, the response came quickly: "I want to know Him, too." The effect of this acceptance by her friend brought such a sense of God's reality and nearness to this college student as she had never dared to expect. "I knew God must truly be real to me," she said, "or I never could have made Him real to my friend—then it all came over me—the sense of His presence." If only we could hold on to this secret we should find a new joyousness and sense of reinforcement in our life. It is as our Lord said: "Where two or three are gathered together in my name, there am I in the midst of them," and "Go make disciples . . . and lo! I am with you all the days even unto the end of the world" (Matt. 18 : 20 and 28 : 19, 20).

There is no end to the relationship of love. If we have in love helped another to find in Jesus Christ the secret of peace and power to live victoriously, we will surely be ready to protect that life and help it to full fruition. This will involve our "standing by" in sympathy when some sudden fiery test comes; it may mean a letter when one is facing an untried experience, a word of courage or confidence, a time of intercession, a chance for special service, or bringing to that life the comradeship of a new friend who can help. In short, we will show in our relationship the marks of love and help to bring a little nearer the answer to that prayer of our Lord: "That they may all be one . . . and the world may believe that thou didst send me" (John 17 : 21).

Lastly, we must help those to whom we are spiritually related to see that a Christian life means that the process of growth must be continuous, "first the blade, then the ear, then the full corn in the ear." We must expect our desires, our scale of values, our vision of the intellectual reaches of the spiritual life to change and broaden and be part of a larger perspective; but the centre and source of our life in Jesus Christ will never change. If people are "rooted and grounded in Him," we must help them to realize that there will be no limit to the new life and its new perceptions as they live in our Father's world and enter into all the heritage of the past and the fresh discoveries of the future. They need to see that their part is to keep themselves in the love of God by yielding Him instant obedience and by keeping heart and mind open for the growing revelation of God.

BIBLE STUDY XVIII
A Growing Christian

I. *God's expectation.*

Read Isaiah 5 : 1-7. Here is a story of the disappointment of God over His people who did not bear the fruit of righteousness in return for all the care and patience and nurture He had bestowed upon them. Note the pathos in the words of verse 4. It is the glory of a vine that it bears fruit; it is profitable for nothing if it does not produce grapes, for there is no other way in which it can be of use. Jesus continues the use of this figure in John 15 : 1-17. What the branch could not do of itself, it can do if it abides in Jesus Christ, the vine. "Apart from me ye can do nothing," says our Lord, but if we are really finding our source of life in Him, God will so cleanse and prune us by His holy discipline that we shall bear *much* fruit and be indeed true disciples. Therefore every Christian is bound to grow and bear fruit or forfeit his union with the vine, Jesus Christ. The cleansing comes through the *word of Christ* (verse 3), and the spirit that flows through the branches into the fruit is *love* (verses 16 and 17).

See Mark 4 : 26-29 and II Peter 3 : 17, 18 for the description of the growing spiritual life. We cannot measure or hasten our growth; all we can do is to fulfil the conditions in preparing the ground and receiving the

SOURCES OF GROWTH

seed and yielding to the care of the husbandman; then the growth comes naturally, "first the blade, then the ear, then the full grain in the ear."

II. *Some means of growth.*

(1) See Acts 2 : 36–39; 16 : 29–34; Matt. 10 : 32, 33; 28 : 19; Mark 1 : 9–11; Romans 6 : 1–4. Here we are shown the privilege of confessing our leal love for Jesus Christ by identifying ourselves with him in the sacrament of baptism. The example of our Lord, His teaching to the disciples, and their preaching to others ought to present an irresistible appeal to all who desire to share in the redemption offered through Jesus Christ. No denominational differences ought to deter us from the open confession of our relation to God symbolized by the rite of baptism.

(2) Read Luke 22 : 14–20; I Cor. 11 : 23–26; John 6 : 52–57. The sacrament of the Holy Communion was instituted by our Lord as a means of helping us to enter into the intimate fellowship with Him with the body of His disciples. Through it our hearts are fed by the renewal of the gift of life as we pledge again our fidelity to Jesus Christ. It is the centre of our devotion to our crucified Lord and the place where we meet as members of the body of Christ in thanksgiving for all He has done for us.

(3) Read Matt. 18 : 19, 20; Acts 12 : 12–17 and 20 : 36–38. One means of spiritual strength is through fellowship in prayer. There is the special promise of the presence of Christ when two or three are meeting in united prayer, and the renewed strength and spiritual vision come as a result. We neglect too often the help that we might have if we prayed often one with another.

(4) See Acts 1 : 8 and I John 3 : 16. The Christian life is a dynamic and we cannot live unto ourselves. We grow and increase in strength only as we share our life with others in some service that releases the power of God in their lives. It is our business to find out the purpose of God for us and give Him our loyal service. It takes time to find our place of service, but we are given wisdom if we are ready with open heart and mind to follow God's guidance. The counsel from Henry Drummond's experience has helped many Christians:

"1. Pray.

"2. Think.

"3. Talk to wise people, but do not regard their decision as final.

"4. Beware of the bias of your own will, but do not be too much afraid of it (God never unnecessarily thwarts a man's nature and likings, and it is a mistake to think that His will is in line of the disagreeable).

"5. Meantime do the next thing (for doing God's will in small things is the best preparation for knowing it in great things).

"6. When decision and action are necessary, go ahead.

"7. Never reconsider the decision when it is finally acted upon; and

"8. You will probably not find out till afterward, perhaps long afterward, that you have been led at all."

Questions for Thought

At what times have I been most conscious of God? Under what conditions have I grown most in my spiritual life during the past year? What are the greatest hindrances to spiritual growth? In what ways would you build up foundations for the Christian life of a young man or woman?

CHAPTER XIX

THE PERILS OF SUCCESS

Eternal vigilance is the price of continuous power in service. We may spend so much time in cultivating other people's gardens that our own runs to weeds. Our success in helping others to know God may blind us to subtle spiritual snares that will rob us of our power. Many an earnest Christian has begun a career of unselfish service for Christ in which evidences of spiritual power and leadership have not been wanting; and the lives of many have been enriched. But after a time the power of God may seem ineffective in the life and all the activities may seem benumbed by a subtle paralysis. The service may go on as usual, but it seems more like marking time than making progress. Fortunate is that one who has the sense to stop at once and take a day off for prayer and self-examination to discover the spiritual foe. This chapter need not have been written if all of us who are busy in Christian work had such days at regular intervals for the good of our souls. It is a necessity for us all, and it is a pity that so many of us have to be driven to it by the shock of some experience rather than by finding this communion with the loving Father the natural result of the eager questioning heart of a humble child.

> "If chosen souls could never be alone
> In deep-mid silence open-doored to God
> No great thing ever had been dreamed or done.
> The nurse of full-grown souls is solitude."
>
> (*Lowell.*)

If we look at the state of our heart we are likely to find any one of a number of foes that has crept in silently.

(1) *Chief amongst these is the snare of self-confidence.* This develops in the wake of successful service. At the beginning we are conscious of our need of guidance and depend upon God in childlike humility. The opportunities for service increase and

we feel the pressure of crowded days. Then it is that we are tempted to forsake our habits of devotion, to let service for others take the place of secret prayer and Bible study. We are thus cut off from the current of power and our service seems rather to manifest self-efficiency than the power of the Spirit. Before we know it we are dazzling people with ourselves rather than imparting life.

(2) *Closely related to the first danger is the temptation to professionalism.* Messages that at first were living and virile may become mechanical and suggestive of cant. They may have been real in our experience years ago but they have become moth-eaten possessions that are packed away in the attic of our hearts. It is so easy to use the accustomed phrases of our past experiences with a glib tongue, especially if people expect us to say something. It is equally easy to speak beyond our experience, using the wisdom of others as the proper counsel for spiritual difficulties. This cant may be manifest in our audible prayers as well as in our conversation, and there is nothing that repels one more quickly or mocks our service more surely. There are Christians who seemed to have stopped growing years ago. Their conception of God is no greater and their spiritual discoveries have no present tense. They have no sympathy with those who are straining every nerve to answer the questions of to-day, for long ago they ceased to "fight the good fight of faith." We dare not be content with our growth in grace without losing our sincerity. The only safety lies in guarding the habits of our secret life.

The measure of honesty with which we face God's truth for our personal needs and purpose to express only that which we experience and learn for ourselves is the measure of our vital message. The word of a life always begets the response of a life.

(3) *As we meet with a measure of success in service we are also likely to be overtaken by a spirit of impatience.* God's Spirit works slowly and thoroughly and much of what is being done is hidden from human sight. In our eagerness to get "quick results," we sometimes expect too much and try to force a hothouse growth. We need to remember that not only is a day as a thousand years in God's sight but "a thousand years as a day." A score of ineffectual attempts to help, and months and years of waiting do not warrant us in ceasing from prayer

and perseverance. The spirit of impatience cuts the nerve of influence.

(4) *Experience in dealing with human nature increases our power of discernment.* We are in danger of letting this gift for analysis of character grow more rapidly than our sympathy for the needs we have discerned. It is so easy to lose hold of the love that "hopeth all things, believeth all things" and that "never faileth." When one takes away the spirit of love from the spirit of discernment, the spirit of criticism alone remains. It is only the truth spoken in love from a compassionate heart that does any one any good. Most people have from time to time a sickening sense of their weaknesses; but they do not often have the comradeship of one who knows these weaknesses and yet in quiet trust refuses to think of them as permanent. There is no greater magnet than the drawing power of an honest, loving friend.

(5) *It is quite possible also to undermine our character if in any way we are betrayed into breaking confidences imparted by others,* or permit these evidences of trust to minister to vanity and self-gratulation. We must cultivate the power of "forgetting those things that are behind," lest future opportunities for service be lost through subtle pride in past achievement. Each new relationship is a fresh adventure unlike any in the past and needs to be met with a humble, reverent spirit. When we begin recounting our past successes even to ourselves we find that we begin to lose the childlike spirit that makes us worthy of being trusted again. Perhaps too we may take it for granted that we know just how to deal with the new opportunity because we had success in the past. This confidence in ourselves and our experience may keep us from seeking fresh guidance and bring us a humiliating failure. We are to remember, however, the wonders of God's part in it all, the way we were led, and the never-failing promise of His presence, in order that our faith in His faithfulness may grow increasingly sure.

(6) *We dare not neglect the sources of our faith,* for a lack of confident trust in the keeping power of God and the watchfulness of the Holy Spirit often proves a snare to the Christian worker. At such times it is easy to yield to the spirit of unbelief and fear and to find ourselves unfitted for further service. Times of success are often followed by temptations to depression and physical reaction. Then too the needs of others and

a sense of responsibility for their welfare press heavily on the mind and heart. Nothing will prevent a depressing physical reaction so effectively as a buoyant faith and glad confidence in God, that He will "keep that which is committed to Him," that the burdens of the heart are His and not ours to carry.

(7) *Another peril which lies in the pathway of successful service is the tendency to usurp God's place as judge of a heart.* We find ourselves slipping into the habit of drawing dogmatic conclusions about people and assuming to question the motive of their hearts. We prejudge a situation and are slow to make full allowance for a changed attitude of mind or growth in spiritual life. This is always keenly discerned by those around us and our chances for help and fellowship are lost. We need to watch and pray daily against this weakness.

(8) *In the beautiful fellowship of sympathetic understanding that we have with those who have been influenced toward the Christian life, a temptation may enter.* We may influence people to depend more on us as workers than on the voice of God in the heart. We may often stand between some one and God. We have not helped another permanently until that one has developed an independent and ever-deepening relation with God. All fellowship in spiritual things should tend to this end. A Christian university student, when asked about the spiritual welfare of another, thus stated the issue tersely: "She gives to others what she should give to God, and she asks of others what she should ask from God." It takes the wisdom of our Lord to know how to have a sincere spiritual fellowship with people and subordinate it all to the influence of God. We generally know by instinct when we are accepting for ourselves what by right belongs to God.

(9) *We need also to watch out for the temptations that come at the time of reaction after a period of successful service.* Morbid thoughts are likely to result from physical weariness and mental fatigue, and earnest Christians often fail to discern the true cause and the remedy. The teachings concerning the unity of spirit, mind, and body show us how dependent each is upon the others; when the body suffers the reaction on mind and spirit is inevitable, and the reverse is also true. One of the common experiences of Christians at such times is the temptation to look back on past guidance of God with uncertainty of conviction. Such questions as these come to us:

"Did I do as I should have done about that particular opportunity?" "The results have not been those I anticipated; was I right in thinking that I was following the will of my Lord?" Many a Christian has been shorn of strength and fitness for further service by yielding to these suggestions. They remind us of the subtle suggestion of the serpent in the Garden of Eden: "Yea, hath God said?" We need rather to think of Paul's imagination when overwhelmed by these doubts: "Wherefore, forgetting those things that are behind and reaching forward, I press on toward the mark." The present opportunity only is ours, the past is beyond our control. God holds us responsible for following the light that is shed on the present and future, confident that our steps are "ordered of the Lord and he delighteth in our way."

In conclusion, the Christian worker will feel daily the pressure of criticism from some who regard religious work as an impertinence and from Christians who do not share the sense of personal responsibility for the welfare of others. Many people are afraid of any sign of religious enthusiasm and dislike what seems unconventional. They are, in reality, too timid to make a spiritual venture or to pay the price of a life of faith; but they extract a virtue from their weakness in the comforting thought that they are "naturally conservative." It is not easy to be free and spontaneous in such an atmosphere, and the temptation to dilute our message and conform to accepted traditions often robs us of spiritual power. The fear of seeming "eccentric" or "old-fashioned" or "narrow" or "emotional" inhibits us all more than we know, and most of us are so sensitive to the conventional restraints of the well-bred religious point of view that we are tempted to forego simplicity and naturalness. It takes a resolute purpose and an intensive study of the life of our Lord to go on simply and quietly, against the tide of human opinion if need be. The joy of leading another to know Jesus Christ makes every struggle against temptation worth while.

There are thousands of people who have never heard the message of Jesus Christ interpreted in human ways through daily fellowship with their friends. If they are ever to hear it we shall have to be true to those things that we have seen and experienced and be willing to share them with our friends. The more natural we are the better we shall succeed. If we value at all our experience with God and our relationship to Jesus Christ, we shall find it more difficult each day to keep it to ourselves.

"That which was from the beginning, which we have heard, which we have seen with our eyes, which we have looked upon, and our hands have handled, of the Word of Life; ... that which we have seen and heard declare we unto you, that ye also may have fellowship with us; and truly our fellowship is with the Father, and with his Son Jesus Christ" (I John 1 : 1-3).

BIBLE STUDY XIX

The Secret of Power

I. *Power within.*

See II Cor. 12 : 6-10. Strength in weakness. God sufficient for personal inadequacy. The glory of our Christian faith is the fact that human weakness plus God's strength is stronger than any human strength. No thorn in the flesh can hinder God, but it saves us from self-confidence, and pride, and easy contentment with ourselves. In the roll of the heroes of faith are those who "from weakness were made strong," and also "endured as seeing Him who is invisible." It is out of such human inadequacy that God works miracles. When we have reached the limit of the possible, then God does the impossible. Why is it that we are not willing to be weak?

II. *Love triumphing over everything.*

Read Romans 8 : 35-39. Jesus Christ never promised us quiet, easy lives. He promised us His peace in spite of tribulation (John 16 : 33). We know the reality of the peace because it is present when everything conspires to take it away. We know love when it stands by us even though everything else fails. Why is it that people are so slow to believe the word of Christ and test it out? Have we ever been as sure of the unfailing love of God *in* tribulations as Paul was? If not, why not?

III. *The source of power in meeting the need of others.*

Read Mark 9 : 14-29. Here we have the moral dynamic with which to work miracles in the name of Jesus, and this faith comes only through unselfish intercessory prayer. If our power over other lives is limited by our prayer, why do we not look upon prayer as the most essential method of achieving results? There are people all about us who are spiritually inert; who must be helped by some one to get deliverance from their bondage. How is help to come to them unless it is mediated to them through us as channels? Am I willing, through prayer, to pay the price of having power to set captives free and to open blind eyes? Jesus said: "Peace be unto you: as the Father hath sent me *even so* send I you." Let us rise to the challenge, that the burden of proof may rest on the faithful word of our Lord. Our part is to voice Miss Havergal's prayer in all sincerity:

> "Lord, speak to me, that I may speak
> In living echoes of thy tone;
> As Thou hast sought, so let me seek,
> Thy erring children lost and lone.
>
> . . . .
>
> "Oh, fill me with Thy fulness, Lord,
> Until my very heart o'erflow
> In kindling thought and glowing word,
> Thy love to tell, Thy praise to show.
>
> "Oh, use me, Lord, use even me,
> Just as Thou wilt, and when, and where;
> Until Thy blessed face I see,
> Thy rest, Thy joy, Thy glory share."

REFERENCES FOR READING

CHAPTER I

Ward, Harry, *Social Evangelism*.
Rauschenbusch, *The Social Principles of Jesus*.
Coffin, Henry Sloan, *Social Aspects of the Cross*.
Smith, George Adam, *Isaiah, volume II* (Expositor's Bible).

CHAPTER II

James, William, *Talks on Psychology and Life's Ideals*.
Royce, Josiah, *The Philosophy of Loyalty*.
Angus, *Discipleship*.

CHAPTER III

Bushnell, Horace, *Sermons for the New Life*, chapter I, "Every Man's Life a Plan of God."
Bull, *The Missioner's Handbook*, chapter I.
Brooks, Phillips, *Lectures on Preaching*.

CHAPTER IV

Brent, Charles H., *Leadership*.
Pearce, Mark Guy, *The Christianity of Jesus Christ*.
Bull, *The Missioner's Handbook*, chapter II.

CHAPTER V

Payot, *The Education of the Will*.
King, Henry C., *Rational Living*.
James, William, *The Varieties of Religious Experience*.
Foster, *Decision of Character*.

CHAPTER VI

Coe, George A., *The Psychology of Religion*.
Stevens, *The Psychology of the Christian Soul*.
Warner, *The Psychology of the Christian Life*.
King, Henry C., *Personal and Ideal Elements in Education*.
Horne, *Psychological Principles of Education*.

CHAPTER VII

McComb, *The Power of Self-Suggestion*.
Bligh, *The Direction of Desire*.
Sadler, *The Physiology of Faith and Fear*, section 2.

White, *The Mechanism of Character Formation.*
Münsterberg, Hugo, *Psychotherapy.*

CHAPTER VIII

Coe, George A., *A Social Theory of Religious Education.*
Rowland, *The Right to Believe.*
James, William, *Talks on Psychology and Life's Ideals.*
Drummond, Henry, *The New Evangelism.*

CHAPTER IX

Swetenham, L., *Conquering Prayer.*
McFadyen, J. E., *The Prayers of the Bible.*
Fosdick, H. E., *The Meaning of Prayer.*
Jones, Rufus M., *The Double Search.*
Phelps, Austin, *The Still Hour.*

CHAPTER X

Coe, George A., *Education in Religion and Morals.*
Bull, *The Missioner's Handbook,* chapter III.
Law, William, *A Serious Call to a Devout and Holy Life.*
Bunyan, John, *Pilgrim's Progress.*

CHAPTER XI

Bushnell, Horace, *Nature and the Supernatural.*
Glover, T. R., *The Jesus of History.*

CHAPTER XII

Ross, George A. Johnston, *The God We Trust.*
Simpson, Carnegie, *The Fact of Christ.*
Mackenzie, W. Douglas, *The Final Faith.*
Jefferson, Charles E., *Things Fundamental.*
Bushnell, Horace, *The Character of Jesus.*
McConnell, Francis J., *Personal Christianity.*

CHAPTER XIII

King, Henry C., *A Rational Fight for Character.*
Cabot, Richard C., *What Men Live by.*

CHAPTER XIV

Cabot, Ella Lyman, *Everyday Ethics.*
Condé, Bertha, *The Business of Being a Friend.*
Moxcey, Mary E., *Girlhood and Character.*

CHAPTER XV

Coe, George A., *Education in Religion and Morals.*
Warner, *The Psychology of the Christian Life,* part II.

CHAPTER XVI

King, Henry C., *The Seeming Unreality of the Spiritual Life.*
Robinson, Forbes, *Letters to His Friends.*

CHAPTER XVII

Rankin, Mary Everett, *A Course for Beginners in Religious Education.*
Alexander, John L., *The Boy and the Sunday School.*
Neale, J. M., *Sermons to Children.*

CHAPTER XVIII

Brent, Charles H., *With God in Prayer.*
Smith, George Adam, *The Life of Henry Drummond.*

CHAPTER XIX

Spurgeon, Charles H., *Lectures to My Students.*

WITHDRAWN
from
Funderburg Library